Gathering Stones

GATHERING STONES

Remembering All That God Has Done For You

SARA W. BERRY

NASHVILLE

NEW YORK • LONDON • MELBOURNE • VANCOUVER

GATHERING STONES
Remembering All That God Has Done For You

Published in New York, New York, by Morgan James Publishing. Morgan James is a trademark of Morgan James, LLC. www.MorganJamesPublishing.com

Unless otherwise indicated, Scripture quotations are from:
Holy Bible, NEW INTERNATIONAL VERSION®, NIV® Copyright © 1973, 1978, 1984, 2011 by Biblica, Inc.® Used by permission. All rights reserved worldwide.
Other Scripture quotations are from:
(NASB®) New American Standard Bible®, Copyright © 1960, 1971, 1977, 1995 by The Lockman Foundation. Used by permission. All rights reserved. www.lockman.org
New King James Version®. Copyright © 1982 by Thomas Nelson. Used by permission. All rights reserved.
The Holy Bible, Berean Study Bible, BSB. Copyright ©2016, 2018 by Bible Hub. Used by Permission. All Rights Reserved Worldwide.
Scripture quotations marked (NLT) are taken from the Holy Bible, New Living Translation, copyright ©1996, 2004, 2007 by Tyndale House Foundation. Used by permission of Tyndale House Publishers, Carol Stream, Illinois 60188. All rights reserved.

Proudly distributed by Ingram Publisher Services.

Morgan James BOGO™

A **FREE** ebook edition is available for you or a friend with the purchase of this print book.

CLEARLY SIGN YOUR NAME ABOVE

Instructions to claim your free ebook edition:
1. Visit MorganJamesBOGO.com
2. Sign your name CLEARLY in the space above
3. Complete the form and submit a photo of this entire page
4. You or your friend can download the ebook to your preferred device

ISBN 9781631956157 paperback
ISBN 9781631956164 ebook
Library of Congress Control Number:
2021937315

Cover and Interior Design by:
Chris Treccani
www.3dogcreative.net

Morgan James PUBLISHING

Builds

with...

Habitat for Humanity®
Peninsula and Greater Williamsburg

Morgan James is a proud partner of Habitat for Humanity Peninsula and Greater Williamsburg. Partners in building since 2006.

Get involved today! Visit MorganJamesPublishing.com/giving-back

In memory of my mom, Nancy Ann Williams, who prayed me through every hard time and rejoiced with me in every good circumstance; who first taught me to pray and showed me how to follow Jesus through her constant example and unconditional love; who is now cheering me on, first in line of my great cloud of witnesses.

I'll meet you at the Gate!

CONTENTS

ACKNOWLEDGMENTS

Many thanks to all the wonderful folks at Morgan James for publishing this book and for guiding me through the process in such a kind, encouraging, and professional manner.

I am so grateful to Tom Dean for catching the vision for this book and for being a mentor and friend throughout the process.

Thanks also to my friend Mary Jo Tate for her extraordinary editing skills. She makes me a better writer.

To my husband, Mont, and to my ten children (You read that right!), I could never do what I do without your support. I love each of you more than words could ever say.

And to Jesus: "To you alone; to you alone and not to me must glory be given because of your constant love and faithfulness" (Psalm 115:1).

INTRODUCTION

In November of 2012, my husband, Mont, and I stood with our newly adopted son on a pathway that ran between two busy streets in Zhengzhou, China. Each side of the pathway was overflowing with gorgeous red flowers rising from abundant green leaves. It was a beautiful spot. Yet my heart felt heavy, for this was where my son's birth mother, for reasons unknown, decided to release him to an undetermined pathway of life. I like to think that she chose that spot not only because it was beautiful but also because it was well traveled each day, ensuring that he would not stay there for long.

I wasn't convinced that I even wanted to see this place that began my son's history. But after I arrived, I was glad I had come, for an overwhelming sense of peace filled my heart as we stood there. What perhaps would seem to others a sad spot of loss and abandonment was really a finding spot. It was the place where my son was found! As we stood there with loud sounds of traffic on either side and many passersby staring with curiosity at the foreigners holding a young Chinese boy, we prayed aloud. We asked God to redeem this spot of abandonment, and we reclaimed it as a Finding Spot. In the years since then, it has become very evident that the grace of God rewrote the storyline. And such is the case in our own life stories.

What a picture of the beauty of the gospel! Think about it—that place of being abandoned was really a place of being found. And all of us were orphans before being adopted into the family of God. I once was lost, but now I'm found! In the same way, our lost spots are really found spots, our sad spots are our spots of comfort, our weak spots are really spots of His strength being revealed. Romans 8:15 tells us that we are adopted by God as heirs. We did not receive a spirit of fear but of sonship, and by that we cry Abba Father—Daddy! We are chosen, not abandoned.

This memory always strikes me with profound gratitude for what God has done in my life. You see, it is always important to remember what God has done. There were many times in the Bible when believers gathered stones to pile up as reminders of the great truths of God's power and grace. Remembering is a conscious act—an effort that provides great reward for our souls. Deuteronomy 4:9 (NLT) says, "But watch out! Be careful never to forget what you yourself have seen. Do not let these memories escape from your mind as long as you live! And be sure to pass them on to your children and grandchildren."

Why is remembering so important that people in the Bible gathered stones as reminders? I believe it is because we are forgetful. We forget who God is and what He has done for us. We need that tangible reminder to push through when times are hard. Even the prophet Samuel needed a tangible reminder. We see in 1 Samuel 7:12 that he gathered his own stone of remembrance and named it Ebenezer, which means "Thus far the LORD has helped us."

How much more clearly this verse helps us understand the meaning the second verse of that beautiful old hymn, "Come Thou Fount of Every Blessing":

> Here I raise my Ebenezer;
> Hither by Thy help I'm come;
> And I hope, by Thy good pleasure,
> Safely to arrive at home.
> Jesus sought me when a stranger,
> Wandering from the fold of God;
> He, to rescue me from danger,
> Interposed His precious blood.[1]

In the coming weeks, we will gather our own stones of remembrance. Our journey through this book will take us through a process of remembering. This remembering will be divided into five sections:

- Remembering Why We Must Remember: Days 1–5
- Remembering Who He Is: Days 6–15
- Remembering What He Has Promised: Days 16–26
- Remembering What He Has Instructed: Days 27–33

- Remembering What He Has Done: Days 34–40

At the end of each devotional, you will find a focus verse and a Scripture-based prayer. I encourage you to jot down those verses and carry them with you or make another effort to hide that Word in your heart. The Bible tells us that the Word is a double-edged sword—powerful, convicting, and transforming. The Word is also our only defensive weapon in the armor of God—Ephesians 6 refers to the sword of the Spirit, which is the Word of God. And Jesus is referred to as the Living Word. As we carry the Word of God in our hearts, we carry Jesus with us. Finally, God created the entire universe with a word. The power of the Word of God will literally change your life as you walk through this journey of remembering.

As we spend the next 40 days gathering stones of remembrance, may the Lord bless us, transform us, and make us ready to better understand the great power of the Risen Savior. And perhaps we will each discover our own Finding Spots.

DAY 1

Remembering Why We Must Remember:

Why Forty Days?

Welcome to Day 1 of a 40-day journey. Before we begin, there is something I believe is important to understand: Why 40?

There are many references in the Bible to certain key numbers. I call them holy numbers. Some of the most common are 3, 7, 12, and 40. The number 3 can be classified as holy perfection like the Trinity—Father, Son, and Holy Spirit. The number 7 indicates completion and perfection—like the 7 days of creation. The number 12 often encompasses the family of God, representing all God's people, and reminds us of the covenant or unending promise of relationship between God and His people— like the 12 tribes of Israel or the 12 disciples. And the number 40 is often a number of cleansing and preparation for the extraordinary.

Remember Noah? How many days did cleansing rain fall to the earth to rid it of wickedness? Yep, it was 40 days and 40 nights. The Israelites wandered for 40 years as they were cleansed and prepared to enter the Promised Land. Even in church traditions, 40 is a significant number as evidenced in the 40 days of Lent, the time of preparation before Easter.

So the answer to "Why 40?" is that we choose to remember for 40 days in order to be cleansed. In order to be transformed. In order to invite the preparation of the Holy Spirit to make our hearts and minds ready for God to do something extraordinary in our ordinary lives.

This bears repeating: God loves to take our ordinary lives and make them extraordinary. Trust Him. Wait and see. Be still and know that He is God. He is with you. He is for you. He wants to show you how lovingly He can transform you and take you to the extraordinary places of His purpose for your life. And it begins with remembering.

Focus Verse: "Create in me a clean heart, O God, And renew a steadfast spirit within me." ~ Psalm 51:10 (NASB)

Focus Prayer: Lord, may we know that You, who began a good work in us, will bring it to completion

until the day of Christ Jesus. In Jesus' Name, amen.
(Philippians 1:6)

DAY 2:

Remembering Why We Must Remember:

Why Be Strong and Courageous?

The Israelites in days of old were a lot like me. They acknowledged God, but they often let their hearts grow hard. They had been miraculously rescued from slavery in Egypt, yet their trust in God quickly failed. They reached the edge of the Promised Land, but they were afraid to go in. They were scared of the giants in the land. They thought they might be safer on the outside looking in than on the inside gathering all that God had promised them.

Only Joshua and his buddy Caleb believed. So the Israelites were punished with a season of wandering. They wandered for 40 years. There's that number again. They needed cleansing. They needed preparation. So that is what God orchestrated on their behalf. In fact, they wandered until the entire unbelieving generation had died off. Caleb and Joshua alone were prepared to lead the next generation into the Promised Land.

When the 40 years were complete, the time had come. I bet God was excited—just like I am when my kids open their presents on Christmas morning. And He had picked just the right person to lead them into the Promised Land. Joshua wasn't perfect, but he had humility of heart.

Joshua is a person to whom I can relate. He outwardly appeared strong and courageous, yet inwardly he must have dealt with fear and insecurity, confusion and discouragement.

In the first chapter of the book of Joshua, we see that God told Joshua three different times to "be strong and courageous." Three different times God reminded Joshua that He would be with him and that He would never leave him or forsake him. And that is just in the first chapter!

Why did God have to tell him to be strong and courageous so many times? I think it is because Joshua was an ordinary man who was called to an extraordinary job by his extraordinary God. And because he was ordinary, just like you and me, he waxed and waned between great seasons of faith, courage, and confidence and fear, doubt, and discouragement.

When he was tempted toward fear and doubt, Joshua knew where to go for help. He continued his faithful obedience to God, listening for instruction and courageously following what God said. Courage is not the absence of fear but the ability to press on despite the fear. And Joshua knew that true courage comes from the Source of all good things—God. Ask God to give you courage today.

Focus Verse: "Have I not commanded you? Be strong and courageous. Do not be afraid; do not be discouraged, for the Lord your God will be with you wherever you go." ~ Joshua 1:9

Focus Prayer: Lord, may we be strong and courageous. Help us not to be terrified or discouraged. May we know that the Lord our God is with us wherever we go. May we be willing to stand for You. In Jesus' Name, amen. (Joshua 1:9)

Remembering Why We Must Remember:

Why Be a Stone Gatherer?

What are the roadblocks in your life? What causes you to stumble in your faith? What trips you up just as you are beginning to run the race of life well?

For the Israelites, the Jordan River was a roadblock. It stopped the progression of the promise. After all the years of wandering, they were so close they could feel it! They could smell it! They were finally at the borders of the Promised Land, but they weren't in it yet.

There was one more river to cross, but it was a doozy! At that time of year, the Jordan River was at flood stage. Maybe a few of the strongest could ford the river, but Joshua had the holy assignment of getting all the people across the flooded waters of the Jordan River—40,000 men, plus women, children, and animals.

They spent three more days consecrating themselves to God, and then it was time. They were ready to cross, ready for God to make the way. They had heard of what He had done in the past, parting the Red Sea. Was it possible He would do it again?

As they approached the Jordan River, it appeared nothing was happening. But then they took that step of faith, allowing their feet to touch the water's edge. They stepped into the flooded Jordan River. And when they stepped out in faith, the waters of the river rolled back, and the people walked forward on dry land. It wasn't even a muddy, murky mess to trudge through. It was solid, dry ground. Were they afraid that the water would fall back on them? Did they run across in fear or walk quickly across in amazement? Regardless of their emotions at the time, they took that step of faith and kept going.

After all were safely across, God gave another assignment. He told Joshua to go back to the middle of the Jordan River and gather 12 stones. These were to be stones of remembrance.

The Lord wanted them to take the stones from the Jordan because He knew they were a forgetful people. They were forgetful about who He is, what He can do, and what He requires. I am forgetful too. That is what this book is all about—remembering instead of forgetting.

And as we remember who He is, what He has done, and what He will do, He will begin to do extraordinary things. Why? So that all will know that God is powerful and wonderful and kind and merciful and loving. When people see us and what God does despite our ordinariness, God alone will be glorified.

Focus Verse: "Not to us, LORD, not to us but to your name be the glory, because of your love and faithfulness." ~ Psalm 115:1

Focus Prayer: Lord, may we trust You with all our hearts, leaning not on our own understanding. In all our ways, may we acknowledge You, and You will make our paths straight. In Jesus' Name, amen. (Proverbs 3:5-6)

DAY 4:

Remembering Why We Must Remember:

Gathering Stones—or Pecans

When my fourth child, Troy, went off to school for the first time, I was surprised at what a hard time I had with that. After all, I had survived the trauma of my first three children heading off to school. You would think that I would be used to it, even a little excited about it, by now.

But I wasn't. I kept wondering if I had made the best use of the time I'd had with him before he ended up being with others more hours of the day than with me. I wanted to know that our sweet relationship was solid enough. Yes, I expected change, but I hoped that that special bond would not leave.

One day when I picked him up from school, he reached into his backpack and showed me a pecan he had found on the playground. I told him how much I loved pecans. They remind me of going to my grandparents' house when I was a little girl. Their four-acre yard was filled with pecan trees, and we spent many hours gathering boxes full of pecans. They even had a special nutcracker that they allowed us to use.

Troy listened patiently and quietly while I reminisced, then continued telling me about his school day. I assumed my words were going in one ear and out the other. However, the next day, and the next, and the next, and for many days afterward, Troy brought me pecans. Soon his backpack was so heavy with these treasures that I had to gently encourage him to spend his recess time playing soccer or climbing on the playground equipment. But secretly, those days of pecan gathering by my precious son brought joy to my heart.

Those pecans were so special to me because he remembered me. I know the reality of friends and studies and teachers—he could go a whole day and not think of me. But when he saw the pecans, he remembered his mom! That meant so much to me. And then I thought: How must our Heavenly Father feel when the busyness of our lives makes us forget Him, who has done so much for us?

That is what gathering stones of remembrance is all about. Joshua gathered the stones from the Jordan River in order to remember. So we must gather stones—or pecans—in order to remember the One who never forgets us.

Focus Verse: "Can a woman forget her nursing child And have no compassion on the son of her womb? Even these may forget, but I will not forget you. Behold, I have inscribed you on the palms of My hands; Your walls are continually before Me." ~ Isaiah 49:15–16 (NASB)

Focus Prayer: Lord, we want to adhere to your warning to be careful and watch ourselves closely so that we do not forget the things our eyes have seen or let them fade from our hearts as long as we live. Help us to teach them to the next generation, as Your Word instructs. We are relying on your strength and wisdom to do that. Thank you, Lord, for all the great and mighty things You have done and will continue to do, even if we don't see them. Thank you for loving us. In Jesus' Name, amen. (Deuteronomy 4:9, Jeremiah 33:3)

Remembering Why:

Forty Days of Remembering

Isaiah 17:10 tells us, "You have forgotten God your Savior; you have not remembered the Rock, your fortress." These words greeted me on the day I was personally reminded once again to remember. As I read my Bible that morning, I heard these faint whisperings in my spirit: "Remember. Remember Who I am. Remember what I told you. Remember what I have done for you."

Once again, I had forgotten. Once again, I feared. Once again, I tried to make everything make sense. Oh, surely He did not mean it that way. Surely there is a way around that commandment, a way to make right—and righteous—that recent action.

But when I sit in His presence, remembering Who He is and what He has told me, I have no justifications to defend or make sense of questions that I have. I only have Him.

And that is enough for now . . . until I forget again. And once again I am called to remember. We must remember who He Is, what He has done, and what He will do.

God told the Israelites to gather stones of remembrance. That is what I am trying to do through this devotional book. I am gathering stones.

When was the last time you picked up a stone? Why not today? Go outside and find one. Or buy a bag of them at your local craft store. Or just gather your own mental stones of remembrance and record them in a journal.

This is a season of remembering, and in the remaining days of this devotional journey, let's remember who He is, what He has promised, what He has instructed, and what He has done.

Focus Verse: "Remember His wonderful deeds which He has done, His marvels and the judgments from His mouth." ~ 1 Chronicles 16:12 (NASB)

Focus Prayer: Lord, I praise you, for I know that by Your mighty power at work within us, You are able to accomplish far more that we could ever hope, dream, or imagine. May you be glorified in the lives of each of your children. In Jesus' Name, amen. (Ephesians 3:20)

DAY 6

Remembering Who He Is:

The Cornerstone

As we gather our own stones of remembrance, we must most of all remember who He is. He is the Chief Cornerstone.

What is a cornerstone? It is also called a foundation stone. The cornerstone is the first stone set in the construction of a masonry foundation. It is the most important stone laid since all other stones are set in reference to the cornerstone. It determines the position of the entire structure.

And so it should be. Jesus, our Chief Cornerstone, should be laid first in our hearts and lives. All other things in our lives should be set in reference to Him. For the Bible says, "See, I lay a stone in Zion, a chosen and precious cornerstone, and the one who trusts in him will never be put to shame" (1 Peter 2:6).

Is Jesus your Chief Cornerstone? Is He first in your heart, your life, and your thoughts? Do you set all else in reference to Him? Pause for just a moment and ask the Holy Spirit to reveal to you anything that has taken precedence over Jesus. Did anything come to mind? If so, lay it down, friend. Offer it as a sacrifice to the Lord.

Often we lay a foundation built on many good things, but only One can be the Chief Cornerstone. No spouse, no job, no dream, no child, no aspiration should take the place of this One. All else will fall into place correctly, if Jesus is laid first in your heart and your life.

Focus Verse: "The stone which the builders rejected Has become the chief cornerstone. This is the Lord's doing; It is marvelous in our eyes." ~ Psalm 118:22–23 (NKJV)

Focus Prayer: Lord, Your Word tells us that we are no longer strangers and foreigners, but fellow citizens with the saints and members of the household of God, having been built on the foundation of the apostles and prophets, You have showed us that Jesus Christ Himself is the Chief Cornerstone and that He will build us up in the Lord so that our lives will be a dwelling place for God. We are humbled that you would want to be with us, and we are grateful that you will never leave us. Thank You, Lord, for Your goodness in our lives. Open our eyes to see it. In Jesus' Name, amen. (Ephesians 2:19–22)

DAY 7

Remembering Who He Is:

King of Kings

Have you ever met a king? I haven't. Have you ever met a president—of anything? I bet you have. Maybe you are the president of something.

A president or king commands respect—some more than others. A king has subjects who are under his authority. A king is royalty, is important, is noticed.

The amount of respect and authority a king has depends upon what he is king of. King of the hill, king of the jungle—the respect or significance depends upon which hill and which jungle he is king of.

Combine all the kings, presidents, and rulers of anything—islands, countries, companies, and PTA organizations. Think about them all together in one place. That is a lot of authority and power.

Now think about *the One* who is above them all—Jesus, the King of all Kings. Jesus is the ultimate authority, the ultimate power, the One who commands the ultimate respect. Now consider that this Ultimate One adores you. Wow!

If I told you that I knew the king of an earthly country, that would make me important, wouldn't it? You would think it was a no-brainer if I kept my appointments with that king and made time for him.

But what about the *King of Kings*, the lover of my soul, Jesus? What about Him? Isn't it logical that I should make time for and spend time with *that* King? Maybe we just forget who He is.

Because if we really remembered, we would make the time, wouldn't we? We would understand the authority and the power, and we would want to be near it.

Focus Verse: "They will wage war against the Lamb, but the Lamb will triumph over them because he is Lord of lords and King of kings—and with him will be his called, chosen and faithful followers." ~ Revelation 17:14

Focus Prayer: Thank You, Jesus—King of all kings—for loving us. Thank You for freeing us from our sins by Your blood and making us a part of Your kingdom. To You be glory and dominion forever and ever. In Jesus' Name, amen. (Revelation 1:5–6)

DAY 8

Remembering Who He Is:

Lord of Lords

I became a Christian as a little girl, when I knelt beside my bed and prayed with my Daddy. I believe God saved me at that point. However, when I was a teenager, I finally understood lordship. I finally understood that Jesus wants to be both Savior of our souls and Lord of our lives.

There is a difference. Having Jesus as Lord over every aspect of our lives involves surrendering our self-reliance and control. Many times, God shows me another area of my life that I have not surrendered to His lordship. He shows me through His Word, through prayer, and through other people. At that point, I confess and pray and surrender yet again.

In the Old Testament we find a little passage with a lot of significance that is easily overlooked. Exodus 21 sets forth the laws regarding Hebrew servants. Every seventh year, the servants had the opportunity to be set free. However, if a servant chose to, he could at that point become a servant for life.

Why would a servant want that? The Bible says that if the servant loved his master and did not want to go free, then the master would take him to the doorpost and pierce his ear with an awl. Then he would be servant for life. That is a beautiful example of lordship. I love Jesus. I don't want to be free of Him or His ways. Only in Him is true freedom found.

Many years ago, I wrote a little poem, which I still often use as a prayer:

> Pierce my ear, O my great King.
> Put in place Your royal ring.
> So all may know and all may see.
> Always, only, I serve Thee.

Today, will you ask Jesus, your *Lord* and Savior, if there is anything you are holding back from Him? He will gently and lovingly reveal those things and give you the strength to truly make Him Lord of all aspects of your life.

Focus Verse: "Therefore God exalted him to the highest place and gave him the name that is above every name, that at the name of Jesus every knee should bow, in heaven and on earth and under the earth, and every tongue acknowledge that Jesus Christ is Lord, to the glory of God the Father." ~ Philippians 2:9–11

Focus Prayer: Thank You for your great promise of salvation. We know that if we confess with our mouths that Jesus is Lord and believe in our hearts that God raised Him from the dead, we will be saved. Restore unto us the joy of our salvation. In Jesus' Name, amen. (Romans 10:9, Psalm 51:12)

DAY 9

Remembering Who He Is:

The Holy One

The inner court of the temple of the Israelites was called the Holy of Holies. It was the place where God, the King of Kings, dwelt. It was so holy that no one could stand in the inner court, lest he die. Once a year, the high priest went into the inner court to offer a sacrifice for the sins of the people. A rope was tied around his ankle so that he could be pulled out of the inner court if he died there.

The Holy of Holies was separated from the rest of the temple by a great curtain, very high and very thick. We are told in Scripture that the day Jesus died on the cross, this mighty curtain ripped from top to bottom. It was too high and too thick for a man to rip it. Our Christian faith maintains that it was ripped by God, symbolizing that we can now come boldly to the throne of grace because of the sacrifice that was made on our behalf.

We can now rejoice in our readily available access to God. And we should go boldly to Him, unafraid, confident in the love of the Father.

But let's not take this great gift lightly. Let's not forget the great cost paid so that we can boldly approach Him. It is only when we stand covered by the shed blood of Christ that we can stand at all before such a holy God.

God has not changed. He is as holy as He ever was. What has changed is our covering. What has changed is our "access pass" bought with such a great price. Praise Jesus today for His gift of grace.

Focus Verse: "There is no one holy like the LORD; . . . there is no Rock like our God." ~ 1 Samuel 2:2

Focus Prayer: Lord, You are holy. We call out to one another and say, "Holy, holy, holy is the Lord of hosts; the whole earth is full of his glory!" Help us, Lord, to become more like You, because it is written, "Be holy, because I am holy." Thank you for cleansing us and restoring us so that we may become holy too. In Jesus' Name, amen. (Isaiah 6:3, 1 Peter 1:16)

DAY 10

Remembering Who He Is:

The Savior

I remember when our first daughter, Katie, was in the sleeping bag phase. She really wanted to sleep with us, but we didn't allow her because truth be told, our double bed comfortably slept only two. So the closest that she could finagle was sleeping in the hall outside our room in her sleeping bag. This sleeping bag phase lasted for a year and a half, which was fine with both mother and child because her room was always neat and I didn't have to wash her sheets!

Our nightly bedtime routines took place in the hallway. One night, as I was tucking her in (as much as is possible with a sleeping bag), she asked me to tell her a missionary story. She loved to hear the true tales of our experiences on the mission field. So I told her the story of a jungle boy who loved Jesus. Toward the end of the story, she interrupted me with an odd question: "Mama, how does he get in there?" Racking my brain about the story, I wasn't sure what she was asking: How does the boy get in the jungle? How does he get in his hut? So I asked her what she meant. She replied, "How does Jesus get in your heart?"

I explained that you ask Him to enter your heart, you tell Him you are sorry for all of the things that you do wrong, and you ask Him to make you into a new creation. She quickly replied, "But . . . how does He get in there?" I thought for a moment and then replied with a question. "Katie, when you are outside playing on a windy day, do you see the wind?" "No, ma'am." "But can you feel the wind on your face? Can you see the trees blowing in the wind?" "Yes, ma'am." "That is what it is like to have Jesus in your heart. You can't see Him enter, but once He does, you feel His presence, and you see that He is working in your life."

We continued our nighttime routine: singing, hugs, water, etc. Just as I was about to leave the hallway, Katie quietly but firmly said, "I want to do that, Mama. I want to ask Jesus into my heart." So I returned to kneel beside her sleeping bag and led her in the prayer for salvation. As soon as she prayed, she joyfully exclaimed, "I get it, Mama! It's like the song." And she began to sing a heartfelt rendition of the beautiful song:

I have decided to follow Jesus.
I have decided to follow Jesus.
I have decided to follow Jesus.
No turning back, no turning back.
Though none go with me, still I will follow.
Though none go with me, still I will follow.
Though none go with me, still I will follow.
No turning back, no turning back.

As I left the hallway, I was overcome with the privilege I had just experienced. I was there when she was born into this earth, and I was there when she was born again.

Jesus is the Savior of the world. He wants to be your Savior. Do you know him as Savior?

Focus Verse: "The LORD lives! Praise be to my Rock! Exalted be God my Savior!" ~ Psalm 18:46

Focus Prayer: Lord, thank you for being our Rock of Salvation. May we help lead others to know You as their Lord and Savior. May we be taught of the Lord so that our peace would be great. Help us to continue to grow in the grace and knowledge of You. May we glorify You both now and forever. In Jesus' Name, amen. (Isaiah 54:13, 2 Peter 3:18)

DAY 11

Remembering Who He Is:

Wonderful Counselor

Have you ever been to see a counselor? Maybe it was a professional therapist. Maybe it was a kind pastor or a wise friend. I certainly have had times in my life when I needed a counselor—during times of grief when I needed someone to share the load with me. One of my closest friends is a counselor. She counsels me so many times and doesn't charge a penny. I am so grateful for her.

We all need a counselor at times in our lives. I always advise friends to seek help and encouragement as needed. But the best counselor of all is Jesus. That is one of His names—Wonderful Counselor. That is who He is—our best, wisest friend, the only One who can see the beginning to end of our life experiences. If we diligently seek the

Wonderful Counselor, our load will be lighter, our troubles milder. But we must seek Him. We must ask for His wise counsel.

I challenge you (and myself) to pick a day (or even just an hour or two) in the next month to devote to the Wonderful Counselor. On this day, spend your free time exclusively with Him, whatever that looks like to you. Don't answer unnecessary phone calls if you can avoid it. Read your Bible, listen to worship music, write a letter to God, pray out loud, take a walk, and sit in the backyard. Wow! Doesn't that sound great?

I bet God will whisper to you that day. I bet you will learn something you didn't know, feel something you haven't felt in a while. I bet you will be at peace. I bet you will be more focused and better prepared to keep the right perspective and stay on the right road when the race of your busy life begins again.

Focus Verse: "He says, 'Be still, and know that I am God; I will be exalted among the nations, I will be exalted in the earth.'" ~ Psalm 46:10

Focus Prayer: Thank you, Lord, that You will be exalted on the earth, whether we see it or not. Thank You that we can rest in the knowledge that You are in control of every aspect of our lives. Help us to find the time and the mental determination to just be still

and know that you are God. In Jesus' Name, amen.
(Psalm 46:10)

Remembering Who He Is:

Mighty God

This topic had me a bit stumped at first. How do we put into words who God is? How can anyone sum up in in a short chapter what that one word—God—encompasses, much less when the second word—Mighty—is added to it? I prayed that God, my Mighty God, would open my eyes to what that means. Quickly, many Bible stories came to mind.

Elijah defeated 400 prophets of Baal when he called on our Mighty God. Moses watched the Red Sea part when he called on our Mighty God. Lazarus was raised from the dead by a word from our Mighty God. The stormy seas were calmed when our Mighty God simply said, "Peace, be still." All of creation was designed and brought into being by our Mighty God. Joshua led the Israelites into the Promised Land, through the parted waters of the Jordan River, because our Mighty God prepared the way.

But the story that came to my mind over and over was the story of Elisha and his servant found in 2 Kings 6:9-18. Elisha was experiencing great persecution. The evil king was intent on capturing and killing him. The army of the king arrived at night and surrounded the city where he was staying. The next morning, when Elisha's servant got up and saw a whole army with horses and chariots surrounding the city, he was terrified. He ran to Elisha, told him the news, and said, "Oh no, my lord! What shall we do?"

Elisha replied, "Don't be afraid! Those who are with us are more than those who are with them." Then Elisha prayed, "Open his eyes, LORD, so that he may see." Then the Lord opened the servant's eyes, and he saw the hills full of heavenly hosts with horses and chariots of fire all around Elisha. Even though the servant could not see them at first, our Mighty God had sent His angels to protect them. In fact, God had been there all along.

As I prayed that God would open my eyes to what that means, I expected a miraculous answer. After all, I have seen God do miraculous things in my life. I had a particular need, a particular request that I wanted Him to answer right away. I really expected Him to show up and show out so that I could tell others of His mighty answer. But as of this moment, I still don't have the answer. But maybe that is the answer.

Do I trust Him as Mighty God, even when I don't yet see the mountains move? Do I know and believe and love who He is, no matter whether He does what I want Him to do? Do I trust that He is working mightily in my life, even if I can't see it or feel it? Today, let's choose to believe—to know—that He is Mighty God in each of our lives, in our families, in our communities, in this crazy world.

He is Mighty God. May our eyes be open to see this truth.

Focus Verse: "The Lord your God is with you, the Mighty Warrior who saves. He will take great delight in you; in his love he will no longer rebuke you, but will rejoice over you with singing." ~ Zephaniah 3:17

Focus Prayer: Thank You, Lord, that You are for us. Thank You for being our defender, our mighty God, our ever-present help in trouble. Thank you for never leaving nor forsaking us. May we glorify You in every aspect of our lives. In Jesus' Name, amen. (Zephaniah 3:17, Psalm 46:1, Deuteronomy 31:6)

DAY 13

Remembering Who He Is:

The Almighty

We have already remembered that our God is Mighty, but He is also the Almighty. What is the difference? *Mighty* means having great power, skill, strength, or force. *Almighty* means having absolute power.

El Shaddai is one of the names of God. It can be translated "God Almighty," and it means "God of the Mountains." So when we refer to God as Almighty, we are saying He has absolute power and He is God of the mountains.

Read the following verses from Psalm 121:1–3 aloud if you can.

> I lift up my eyes to the mountains—where does
> my help come from? My help comes from the LORD,

the Maker of heaven and earth. He will not let your
foot slip—he who watches over you will not slumber.

In this passage the meanings of the word LORD include
"Almighty, God of the mountains." This is called a song
of ascents. *Ascent* means "the act of going higher." This
Psalm was a song the believers sang when they were on a
pilgrimage.

We are on a pilgrimage, aren't we? We are on a spiritual
journey, longing to get closer and closer to God, because
deep down we know He longs to get closer and closer to
us. We can run to this "God of the mountains" and be safe.

When we see the name *Almighty* in Scripture, it is as
if God is shouting to us, "Come on up here! The view is
great! You will see clearly up here! And the best part is you
can live up here! You can *dwell* here!"

The name *Almighty* is found in the scriptures 48 times.
What is really interesting is that 31 of those times are in
the book of Job. You know the book of Job. The painful
one. The one filled with grief and despair and tragedy. The
one that makes us want to cry out, "Really, God? You've
got to be kidding me! I mean, Job was a godly man. He
was one of Your favorites. Really?!"

Yet it is in that book that the Almighty, the great God
of the mountains, is revealed most of all. He is *almighty*.
And if you are going through grief, or illness, or tragedy,
He cries, "Come up here with Me. It is safe up here. You
can dwell here."

Focus Verse: "'Though the mountains be shaken and the hills be removed, yet my unfailing love for you will not be shaken nor my covenant of peace be removed,' says the LORD, who has compassion on you." ~ Isaiah 54:10

Focus Prayer: Thank You, Lord, that you are not just Almighty for others; You are *our* Almighty God. Thank you that You are the Alpha and the Omega, who is and who was and who is to come. We love you, Lord, and we lift our hearts and minds to You. Thank You for your constant love and faithfulness. May we glorify You this day. In Jesus' Name, amen. (Revelation 1:8, Psalm 115:1)

DAY 14

Remembering Who He Is:

The Prince of Peace

Yani was a wife, mother of three, English teacher, and native Costa Rican. She was my friend. I met Yani while working at a Christian school in Costa Rica. She invited my friend Kelli and me into her home when we were lonely, homesick, young, single girls living in an unfamiliar land. She made us feel that we were part of her family when we were so in need of family, despite the age, language, and cultural differences. Yani spoke to us as friends and was there to lovingly teach us the ways of her country.

Yani often invited us to her home for coffee. This time included sandwiches and sweets, pan dulce or tres leches, and of course, the strong, hot coffee that she craved by three o'clock in the afternoon. We could stomach her coffee only with lots and lots of "leche y azuchar, por favor!" (Milk and sugar, please!) It was during these coffee times that she often opened up her heart with tales of her childhood, dreams for her future and the future of her children, and her faith in God.

She spoke in English, which was a welcome reprieve from the constant struggle to comprehend the beautiful but unfamiliar Spanish language. Though her English was very good, her accent was different enough that we had to listen carefully to understand what she was saying. We listened intently not only to understand but also because we loved her and we knew that she loved us.

One day at coffee time, Yani shared an experience from her life, the memory of which was still both painful and precious. She told us about the time when her daughter became very ill. They rushed her to the hospital and spent a long, difficult night not knowing what the outcome would be. At one point during the night, a compassionate Christian nurse felt compelled to pray with Yani. The words of her prayer were simple: that God would make His presence known to Yani and her family and that He would heal her daughter.

Yani struggled to describe in English the depth of peace that she felt at the moment of that prayer. She said, "When that nurse prayed, I could . . . I could hear the footsteps of Jesus."

The footsteps of Jesus! If we listen, they are all around us. He is walking before us, beside us, and behind us.

The footsteps of Jesus assure us that He is here as Wonderful Counselor, Mighty God, the Prince of Peace and that there'll be no limits to the wholeness he brings. But we must remember to listen carefully and intently—not only to understand but also because we love Him and we know that He really loves us! Listen for His footsteps, and you will surely hear.

Psalm 46:10 says, "Be still, and know that I am God!" (NLT). The New American Standard translation says it this way: "Cease striving and know that I am God." And that is the invitation for you this day: Sit down, be still before the Lord, and listen to Him. Cease all of your striving and know that He is God—the extraordinary, awesome God who is pleased to speak to ordinary souls.

Focus Verse: "Let the peace of Christ rule in your hearts, since as members of one body you were called to peace. And be thankful." ~ Colossians 3:15

Focus Prayer: Lord, help us to not be anxious about anything, but in every situation, by prayer and petition, with thanksgiving, present our requests to You. Thank you for Your promise that the peace of God, which transcends all understanding, will guard our hearts and our minds in Christ Jesus. In Jesus' Name, amen. (Philippians 4:6–7)

DAY 15

Remembering Who He Is:

The Everlasting Father

I was 8½ years old when my brother Martin was born. I felt like he was *my* baby. I dressed and fed him. I have always adored him.

I vividly remember that one Christmas, my dad wanted to give Martin a very special present. He wanted to build him a tree house. He worked on it every night for weeks. He would go outside after Martin had gone to bed and begin the difficult work of measuring, sawing, nailing, and sanding. He was so determined to keep the end result as a surprise that each night he would tear down what he had built.

It was as if he were creating a giant puzzle. He would create the pieces, make sure they all fit together, then take them apart until the next day when he would create more pieces, make sure they all fit together, and then take it apart again. Over and over, night after night.

On Christmas Eve, he put all the puzzle pieces in place one last time and fastened them together securely. Then he added one more thing: a very long string that was tied to the tree house and traveled through the backyard, into the house, and through the den, where it was attached on the other end to a wrapped gift. This gift was set aside from the others, waiting for the perfect time to reveal its surprise.

On Christmas morning, we all enjoyed the chaos of opening presents, oohing and aahing over what we had received. Finally, the time for the big reveal had come. This was the last present to be opened, and though it was not for me, it is the only one I remember from that Christmas.

I can still see Martin's face as he began following the string. He was still in footie pajamas, and my mother had insisted that he add his big puffy coat on top. We all gathered behind him as he followed the string to the tree house. It was a little boy's dream come true.

Sometimes there are seasons in our lives when we feel that just like the tree house, we are being torn down over and over again. It is a long, painful process. But if we understand that God is our Everlasting Father, we will realize that each time we are torn down, He is using that as a puzzle piece in a great creation. We must trust Him as the Perfect Father, knowing that He will never allow anything to happen to us that can't be worked for our good.

He is creating a masterpiece out of the pieces of our lives. We must trust the love of our Everlasting Father.

Focus Verse: "For we are God's masterpiece. He has created us anew in Christ Jesus, so we can do the good things he planned for us long ago." ~ Ephesians 2:10 (NLT)

Focus Prayer: Lord, we see what great love You have lavished on us, that we should be called children of God! And that is what we are! What joy this truth brings. Thank You for loving us, dying for us, and adopting us into Your family. In Jesus' Name, amen. (1 John 3:1)

DAY 16

Remembering What He Has Promised:

Salvation

I believe that our life in Christ is a journey—a wonderful, amazing, journey that lasts our entire lives. However, we simply cannot experience the journey if we have not begun the relationship that leads us on the journey. This journey begins upon salvation and is fueled by making our personal relationship with God the highest priority. Just as in any relationship, there will be highs and lows.

An important time in my spiritual walk came when I realized that just because that good feeling went away, it didn't mean Jesus went away. In Joshua 1:5, God says, "I will never leave you nor forsake you."

I have been a Christian for more than 40 years, and I have always found that verse to be true.

Do you remember when you first became a Christian? Even if you were very young, you can have stones of remembrance of the times the joy of your salvation was almost tangible.

Today, I want us to remember and pray one verse in particular:

> Create in me a pure heart, O God, and renew a steadfast spirit within me. Do not cast me from your presence or take your Holy Spirit from me. Restore to me the joy of your salvation and grant me a willing spirit, to sustain me. (Psalm 51:10–12)

Over and over throughout the day, pray, "Restore to me the joy of Your salvation."

May the Lord once again give you the joy that comes from knowing you have been bought with a great price, from knowing He counted you worthy to die for, from knowing that you will live forever with Him, abundantly on this earth and eternally in heaven.

Bask in that joy today. And then go and share it with someone else.

Focus Verse: "Create in me a pure heart, O God, and renew a steadfast spirit within me. Do not cast me from your presence or take your Holy Spirit from me. Restore to me the joy of your salvation and grant me a willing spirit, to sustain me." ~ Psalm 51:10–12

Focus Prayer: Thank you, Jesus, that Your work on the cross provided the path to eternity. Thank you that You give us not only eternal life in heaven but also a fulfilled life on earth. Though the enemy of our soul comes to steal, kill, and destroy, You came that we might have life and have it abundantly. We praise You for Your goodness and faithfulness. In Jesus' Name, amen. (John 10:10)

DAY 17

Remembering What He Has Promised:

The Holy Spirit

I love the Holy Spirit.

Sometimes we don't give that wonderful part of the Trinity enough attention. I once read that most denominations tend to lean toward one part of the Trinity over the others. Some denominations may relate more to the holiness and divinity of God the Father. Others may relate more to the human love of God the Son, Jesus. Still others may relate more to the power and wonder of the Holy Spirit.

Yet it is true that they are all *one*. Three in One. I believe the best balance is equal love, devotion, and attention to all three, for all are our *one* God, the great I Am.

When I was a teenager, I learned the power of daily surrender. I learned to ask the Holy Spirit to blow as a rushing wind through my heart and life. I learned that surrendering to the power of the Holy Spirit empowered me to do all that God had planned for me to do and equipped me to handle anything that life could throw at me.

Scripture tells us that the Spirit is our Comforter, our Counselor, and our Conviction. It says that the Spirit will guide us into all truth. It tells us the Spirit intercedes for us in ways we can't understand. The Holy Spirit stands in the gap on our behalf.

Scripture also says we can grieve the Holy Spirit. May it not be so today. Today may we walk in communion with the Holy Spirit as He moves us along the path of the extraordinary.

Focus Verse: "I will ask the Father, and He will give you another Helper, that He may be with you forever." ~ John 14:16 (NASB)

Focus Prayer: Thank you for sending us the Helper, the Holy Spirit. I pray that we will listen to the Spirit's guidance and that we will hear a voice behind us saying, "This is the way; walk in it." Thank you that the Holy Spirit will guide us to all truth. In Jesus' Name, amen. (John 14:16, Isaiah 30:21, John 16:13)

DAY 18

Remembering What He Has Promised:

Covenantal Love

One of the greatest promises of God is His covenantal love. Yet it can be hard for many Christians to understand. Why is that? Because we often don't truly understand what *covenant* means. Covenantal love means that God has made a never-ending promise to love us no matter what—through thick and thin, good and bad. He will not break His covenant with us. This is amazing truth, almost too big to grasp. Though we were created for eternity, our human minds may find eternal love hard to fathom. We aren't there yet. So the never-ending faithfulness of a covenantal relationship may be hard to understand.

Kay Arthur writes:

> To understand covenant is . . . to discover a promise that has been there all the time, hidden in vague shadows and blurred by the veil of my ignorance. To understand the intimacy and intricate details of God's plan and purpose. To know that because of His covenant of grace I can be assured that I will always be beloved of God. It frees us to bask in His love and to move through every circumstance of life in the security of His promises.[2]

The great missionary to China, Hudson Taylor, understood covenant. When he was down to his last 25 cents, he confidently said, "Twenty-five cents . . . plus all the promises of God!"[3] And God did provide for him and his ministry, which is still thriving after three generations.

Horatio Gates Spafford understood covenant when he penned the beautiful hymn "It Is Well with My Soul" just after he learned that he had lost four of his children to a storm at sea.

My friend Maxie Dunnam understood covenant when he said goodbye to a dear friend, sick with terminal cancer. As Maxie left the room, both knew that they would not see each other again on this earth. His very weak friend raised his hand in farewell and said, "Until tomorrow!"

Understanding covenant gives us extra joy in the good times and extra strength and peace in the bad times. Understanding covenant means that we are never afraid that God will leave us or forsake us. He can't and He won't.

Focus Verse: "'For the mountains may be removed and the hills may shake, But My lovingkindness will not be removed from you, And My covenant of peace will not be shaken,' Says the Lord who has compassion on you." ~ Isaiah 54:10 (NASB)

Focus Prayer: Thank You, Lord, for your never-ending promises. Thank You that You are the Covenant Keeper. Thank You that You will never leave me nor forsake me. Grant me power to keep my covenant with You, Lord. Make me faithful in Your sight, for I know that no temptation has seized me, except what is common to man. Thank You for providing a way out for me in the midst of every temptation. In Jesus' Name, amen. (Deuteronomy 31:6, 1 Corinthians 10:13)

DAY 19

Remembering What He Has Promised:

Forgiveness

Scripture tells us, "Blessed is the one who does not walk in step with the wicked or stand in the way that sinners take or sit in the company of mockers, but whose delight is in the law of the LORD, and who meditates on his law day and night" (Psalm 1:1–2).

Notice the progression of the action words in the first sentence. Think about this contrast between the blessed man and the wicked man. A wicked man will first walk near wickedness, then decide to just stand there, then find himself sitting among the wicked—right at home as one of them! That is a lot like the progression of sin. First, we walk near it, thinking it won't affect us. Then we pause. We stand there close by taking it in but not really participating, but before we know it, we are sitting there smack in the middle of a sinful situation.

Maybe we never intended to sit there, but we do. Why? Because the first mistake we made did not seem so bad. But it started the downward spiral. It made our hearts a bit harder. We failed to delight in the law of the Lord, and we did not meditate on it day and night. We should have run away from the sin at the first conviction. We should not have rationalized it away.

So what are we to do with this human plight? First, we must realize we are all sinners saved only by the grace of God. We all have moments of sin, whether the rest of the world ever knows about it or not. We all must repent.

What does it mean to repent? To turn around and go in the opposite direction. It starts with confession and ends with embracing the power of the cross of Christ, which gives us the power to change. Do you need to repent today? I do.

Though the title of today's reading declares that it is about forgiveness, we have spent most of our time discussing the progression of sin and the need to repent. Why is that? It is because we can't fully understand, embrace, nor appreciate the forgiveness that is offered to us unless we understand our need for it. If we compare ourselves to the rest of the world, we may look pretty good. But if we compare ourselves to the standard set before us in the Word of God, we will see that we are much worse than we thought. And without the forgiveness of Christ, our good works would remain filthy rags. Today, let's not only acknowledge the need to repent but also celebrate the incredible gift of forgiveness.

Focus Verse: "If we confess our sins, He is faithful and righteous to forgive us our sins and to cleanse us from all unrighteousness." ~ 1 John 1:9 (NASB)

Focus Prayer: Lord, thank You for the great promise of forgiveness. May we repent of our sins and acknowledge Your forgiveness, which is the only way we can become pure and holy. Thank you that though our sins are like scarlet, you make us white as snow. In Jesus' Name, amen. (Isaiah 1:18)

DAY 20

Remembering What He Has Promised:

Protection

My daily prayers for my family often involve excerpts from my favorite psalm, Psalm 91, which offers these reassuring words:

> Whoever dwells in the shelter of the Most High will rest in the shadow of the Almighty. I will say of the LORD, "He is my refuge and my fortress, my God, in whom I trust." Surely he will save you from the fowler's snare and from the deadly pestilence. He will cover you with his feathers, and under his wings you will find refuge; His faithfulness will be your shield and rampart. You will not fear the terror of night, nor the arrow that flies by day, nor the pesti-

lence that stalks in the darkness, nor the plague that destroys at midday. A thousand may fall at your side, ten thousand at your right hand, but it will not come near you. You will only observe with your eyes and see the punishment of the wicked. If you say, "The Lord is my refuge," and you make the Most High your dwelling, no harm will overtake you, no disaster will come near your tent. For he will command his angels concerning you to guard you in all your ways; they will lift you up in their hands, so that you will not strike your foot against a stone. You will tread on the lion and the cobra; you will trample the great lion and the serpent. "Because he loves me," says the Lord, "I will rescue him; I will protect him, for he acknowledges my name. He will call on me, and I will answer him; I will be with him in trouble, I will deliver him and honor him. With long life I will satisfy him and show him my salvation."

This passage has practically saved my life—or at least my mental health—at times. When my husband, Mont, was sick in the hospital with meningitis and we were quarantined from all family and friends, this is the passage that I read aloud over and over. Three days later, when we discovered that our daughter Ellie, who was only seven weeks old, also had meningitis, I once again clung to these verses. I was definitely dwelling in the shelter because I knew that no one and nothing else could help me.

When I was in China or Ecuador or Costa Rica, unable to communicate in those languages, I thought of those verses. When I feel myself overwhelmed with fear for my children, these are the verses that I cling to, that I pray, that I struggle to believe.

And as I meditate on them—*dwell* on them—then I grow in my faith once again and choose to believe, to *know*, that my Almighty Father will never forsake me.

According to Lexico.com, *dwell* means "to live in or at a specified place."[4] Sally and Charlie didn't dwell with us until they became officially ours through adoption. When we become officially God's, He makes His home in our hearts. He lives in us and we live in Him. We dwell in His heavenly realm, even while we are on this earth. And it is the only truly safe place.

As I studied the word *dwell*, I also saw another meaning in the phrase *dwell on* regarding the eyes or attention: "linger on a particular object or place." When we dwell on Christ—focusing our thoughts, our eyes, our attitudes, our attention on Him—then we are living in His shelter. That is how we stay in that safe place.

Dwell in His presence today. You will be safe and secure.

Focus Verse: "Whoever dwells in the shelter of the Most High will rest in the shadow of the Almighty. I will say of the LORD, 'He is my refuge and my fortress, my God, in whom I trust.'" ~ Psalm 91:1–2

Focus Prayer: Thank you, Lord, for being our safety, our stronghold in times of trouble, and our refuge and strength. May we dwell in your shelter each day, knowing that no weapon formed against us shall prosper. In Jesus' Name, amen. (Psalm 9:9, Psalm 91:1, Isaiah 54:17)

DAY 21

Remembering What He Has Promised:

Heaven

Do you fear death? Many of us do. I don't really fear death itself, but I do sometimes fear dying. But that is one thing we have in common with every person on the face of the earth: we will all die. We can't get around that fact. But we do have a choice as to whether we are faithful unto death—faithful no matter what our death looks like, be it illness, old age, or persecution. We must remain faithful unto death.

My grandmother was one of the sweetest, most godly women I have ever met. She was diagnosed with bladder cancer when she was eighty years old. I felt cheated. Until the cancer, she looked and acted much younger. I envisioned trips together, holidays, and visits with her great-grandchildren. Yet death came knocking.

One day, about two weeks before she died, my mother and my sister were in the hospital room with her. My sister has a beautiful singing voice, and my grandmother always cherished hearing her sing. So Grandmama requested that my sister sing "Amazing Grace" to her.

As my sister sang, my grandmother closed her eyes. The look on her face was that of peace and amazement. As strange as it sounds, God gave her a picture of heaven. When she closed her eyes, she saw light and life and love. She saw loved ones long passed. At one point, with her eyes still closed, she said, "Someone's calling me baby." Then she gasped. "Daddy!" she said, her face beaming with joy.

After that, my grandmother was not only unafraid; she was eager to go. Previously, she had selected her blue suit to be buried in. She immediately changed it to her white suit "because everyone was dressed in white."

We all came to the hospital that day, knowing that time was drawing near. We were the ones who were sad and upset, not her. As we all gathered around her, she said, "When your time comes, don't be afraid. It is wonderful there. Rejoice."

My grandmother still had much pain to endure in the next couple of weeks. But she knew where she was going, and that truth, placed front and center in her mind, caused her to be faithful unto death. We will all die. But may we live for Him until the moment we run into His arms.

Focus Verse: "Be faithful, even to the point of death, and I will give you life as your victor's crown." ~ Revelation 2:10

Focus Prayer: Thank you, Lord, for the great promise of heaven. Thank You that one day You will wipe every tear from our eyes. Thank you that in heaven there will be no more death or mourning or crying or pain, for the old order of things will pass away. In Jesus' Name, amen. (Revelation 21:4)

DAY 22

Remembering What He Has Promised:

He Will Supply Our Needs

When my friend Kelli and I were missionaries in Costa Rica, our primary responsibility was to teach English in a Costa Rican school. But our true mission turned out to be our work on Saturdays in Los Guidos, a refugee camp outside of San José. There we would simply show up with a Bible lesson and a craft and go from door to door inviting the children to join us. We met under a large tree in the center of the camp.

The homes there consisted of pieces of wood or tin thrown together to make shacks with dirt floors. The children were very poor, and often hungry and dirty. One day in particular, God revealed His grace, mercy, and power in an awesome way. We had been going every Saturday for a couple of months, and we had never had more than 15 children. As we packed the bag of supplies, I carefully counted out enough for 20 craft projects just in case we had a couple of extra children.

To our surprise, as we began the lesson with singing and a Bible story, the children kept coming. I became very nervous about the craft projects, knowing that uncommon luxury was the biggest reason they were coming. As soon as I would finish counting, more children would come. I began to pray furiously as our translator finished up the story. At last count, I realized that 40 children were gathered around the big tree, listening to a story of God's faithfulness.

I didn't know what else to do except to pass out the supplies. I reached into the bag to gather supplies, Kelli reached into the bag to gather supplies, and Ivonnia, our translator, reached into the bag to gather supplies. We kept going back to the bag for more supplies over and over until every child had made a craft project.

After the children left, I looked into the bag once again, and it still contained more supplies. I had packed the bag myself. I knew exactly what was in the bag. I wept when I realized in my heart, not just in my head, that our Lord is the same yesterday, today, and forever. The same Lord who blessed and multiplied the fish and the loaves multiplied our supplies that day. And though those 40 children will never know of the miracle that day, I will never forget.

Focus Verse: "And my God will meet all your needs according to the riches of his glory in Christ Jesus." ~ Philippians 4:19

Focus Prayer: Thank You, Lord, for being trustworthy. May we trust in You with all our hearts and lean not on our own understanding. May we acknowledge You in all our ways, and may we trust You to make our paths straight. In Jesus' Name, amen. (Proverbs 3:5-6)

DAY 23

Remembering What He Has Promised:

He Will Contend

I have had a hard time surrendering my children to the Lord. My reluctance has been based in fear. I guess it took me a few years to really believe that God loves them more than I do. It took me a while to really trust God with my children, no matter what.

I remember the point of surrender with my kids. I was at Pickwick Lake, and I felt overcome with a case of the what-ifs. The more I thought about the future, the more fearful I became. I remember praying a desperate cry for help. I got my Bible and prayed, "Lord, I need a word from You. I need a word from You that I can hang onto." Though I don't really recommend this method, I simply opened my Bible, and the first passage I saw was this:

> As the rain and the snow come down from heaven, and do not return to it without watering the earth and making it bud and flourish, so that it yields seed for the sower and bread for the eater, so is my word that goes out from my mouth: It will not return to me empty, but will accomplish what I desire and achieve the purpose for which I sent it. (Isaiah 55:10–11)

I prayed, "Yes, that is true. God's word will not return void. And I do pray God's Word over each of my children. But Lord, I need a word from You that is specific to them. Give me a word for my children." I flipped a couple of pages and my eyes fell upon the following verse:

> I will contend with those who contend with you, and your children I will save. (Isaiah 49:25)

I immediately felt an overwhelming peace flood my soul. The fear fled. The calm returned. I prayed, "OK, Lord. I believe you. Help me with my unbelief." And whenever Satan tries to bind me again with fear concerning my children, I let my powerful God contend with the enemy, and I simply remember and believe.

A few months after this word from the Lord came to me, my family attended a revival at First Presbyterian Church in Corinth, Mississippi. The speaker offered a time to come to the altar if anyone wanted to receive Christ as Savior and Lord. All of a sudden my son Joseph jumped up, grabbed my hand, and began pulling me down the aisle, all the while encouraging his cousin Rebekah to go too. As I made my way down the aisle with my son to pray, these precious words from the Lord came to my mind: "I will contend with those who contend with you, and your children I will save."

A couple of years later, we had a bit of a scare with Joseph. I had to take him to get a CAT scan of his brain because he was experiencing a lot of dizziness. I remember fighting off the what-ifs and praying instead, "Lord, I gave him to you a long time ago. I will not take him back now." In the end, all was well, but at the time, that was a difficult prayer to pray. You see, it is very hard to surrender something to the Lord and not pick it back up again. But we must remember that His promises are true. He will contend for us.

Focus Verse: "I will contend with those who contend with you, and your children I will save." ~ Isaiah 49:25

Focus Prayer: Thank You, Lord, that You contend for us. We are convinced that You are able to guard what we have entrusted to You. We praise You that You who began a good work in us and our families will bring it to completion. In Jesus' Name, amen. (Isaiah 49:25, 2 Timothy 1:12, Philippians 1:6)

DAY 24

Remembering What He Has Promised:

Guidance

I was new to the country, new to the language, new to public transportation. I had to catch the public bus in San Francisco Dos Rios on the east side of San José, Costa Rica, and take a 30-minute bus ride to Hatillo Dos on the west side of San José. I saw many things that were different from my culture . . . including chickens riding with their owners on the bus. I was a nervous wreck about the whole public bus situation.

What if I got on the wrong bus? I had that experience in another country, and I did not want to go through that again. What if I got off at the wrong stop? How do you even say "bus stop" in Spanish? With the bus being so crowded, what if I couldn't get to the front of the bus in time to get off, if indeed I guessed the correct stop?

So many fears surfaced as I waited for the bus to arrive. The first few days were spent dreading the ride to work. But that all changed in an instant when I saw it . . . the cross. There was a cross on the roof of the church where I taught English. The positioning of the building and the height of the steeple made the cross stand out above all the other buildings packed closely together. I could still see the cross even when I was far away.

I found that once I saw the cross, I only needed to keep my eyes focused on it, and then I would not miss my stop. But even after I learned the secret of the cross, I could still end up on the wrong road if I got distracted and did not keep my eyes on it.

That cross became a great comfort to me. I no longer dreaded the journey. I began to feel confident riding the bus, even experiencing the culture, all because of the cross.

I still felt like a foreigner. I loved the country, loved the experience of living among those beautiful people, but I still did not totally fit in. But I had found contentment with where I was, and I had found the way to overcome my fears so that I could really enjoy and savor what little time I had in Costa Rica.

One day, I was riding along, looking for the cross, and when I saw it, I felt a wave of relief: Yes, there it is! I am going in the right direction! And with those thoughts came the next: This reality in the physical sense was also reality in the spiritual sense. The longing I felt when I was looking for the cross was so like the longing I felt when I was looking for the bearer of the true cross.

Focus Verse: "Let us fix our eyes on Jesus, the author and perfecter of our faith, who for the joy set before Him endured the cross, scorning its shame, and sat down at the right hand of the throne of God." ~ Hebrews 12:2 (BSB)

Focus Prayer: Thank You, Lord, that we can look up and find our help, for our help is from You, Lord, the maker of heaven and earth. Thank you that You will not let us slip, that you guard us day and night, and that You keep us from all harm. Watch over our lives, Lord. Watch over our coming and going both now and forevermore. In Jesus' Name, amen. (Psalm 121:1-8)

Remembering What He Has Promised:

New Creations

Springtime burst forth in my own life one year in a dramatic way. In the late 1980s and early 1990s, I taught first grade at a small Christian school in Memphis, Tennessee. The children were a great source of joy to me, and I often learned more from them than they did from me. I had been teaching them in our daily devotions to pray about everything, and I explained that God did indeed hear and answer our prayers. I frequently allowed different students to come forward in the class and pray aloud for the concerns we had discussed. As is often the case, my lessons were soon put to the test.

A precious little blond girl whom I will call Allie came to class one morning with a beautiful butterfly in a jar. We all oohed and aahed over its magnificent colors. Allie was quick to point out to everyone that it had a broken wing. I could plainly see that a large portion of one wing was not just broken but completely torn off. We placed the jar with the butterfly on the shelf so that everyone could see it. It remained there for most of the morning.

During my break, I went to the prayer room at the church. I locked the door, knelt before my Lord, and poured out my heart. You see, I was in a winter stage of my life—one of those cold, lonely times when we can't see clearly how God could possibly bring about all those great and wonderful things that He promises to those who believe and follow Him. I don't even remember all of the details of that hard time, and it has been so completely healed that the pain is only a distant memory now. On that day, however, I felt pain and confusion so greatly that I spent my entire break kneeling before the Lord, begging to know His presence in my life.

When I returned to the classroom, we began our Bible lesson. One of the children suggested that we pray for Allie's butterfly. Not wanting to retract my admonition that we should bring every concern before the Lord in prayer, I consented. When I asked for volunteers to come forward to pray aloud for the butterfly, three-fourths of the class quickly stepped to the front. As the children began to pray, my heart started racing. I shot up silent prayers like "Lord, get me out of this! Give me wisdom in explaining this to these dear children!" You see, the faith-filled prayers of those first graders were "Lord, please heal the butterfly!" and "Please help the butterfly to fly again!"

When all had prayed and were returning to their seats, one little boy suggested that we let the butterfly get some fresh air. Why I consented I will never know, but before I even realized what was taking place, the whole class had gone out to the grassy courtyard right outside our classroom. When Allie emptied the butterfly from the jar onto the grass, I felt immediate regret for allowing this to take place. It just jumped around—a pitiful sight. I quickly ushered the children back inside, leaving the butterfly in the grass.

I began a math lesson to try to take their minds off the creature, but I kept seeing various children glancing out the window, checking on the still-hopping butterfly. I was in the middle of the very ineffective math lesson when one of the boys stepped away from his seat to look out of the window. He gasped and yelled, "Look!" Everyone rushed from their seats to the window just in time to see the butterfly lift off the ground in flight.

The children began to yell and scream and laugh and cheer and hug, all in pure joy at seeing their prayers answered. One of the other first-grade teachers came in to see what all the commotion was about. All I could do was point out the window at the butterfly, which was now flying all over the courtyard. We stood looking in amazement until the butterfly flew over the wall of the courtyard, past our visibility. Then I once again asked for volunteers to pray. Everyone joined in this time—especially me. We thanked God for His miracle of love, healing, and answered prayer.

And my winter season of life began to lift quickly. You see, I felt like a butterfly with a broken wing. I was a Christian. I had already obtained new life, which is so allegorically portrayed through the life of a butterfly. But painful circumstances had rendered me incapable of flying to the heights that God had planned for me. I, too, needed the healing touch of the Great Physician. I needed to see and feel His Presence. And when I surrendered to Him in the prayer room—when I trusted Him despite what I could see—He showed me His Presence in a way that was far greater than I could have ever imagined.

Are you a butterfly with a broken wing? Call upon the Father, the Great Physician, to heal you so that you can fly to the heights of His beautiful plan for your life. Everyone has scars. That is life's reality. That will continue to be life's reality until we head to our heavenly home or Jesus comes back. But scars can fade with proper healing. And no counselor, no self-help book, no medication can heal completely—only Jesus, the Great Physician.

Surrendering to the Lordship of Jesus in every area of your life does not give you a barrier from the pain or the scars. But it does give you automatic access to the Great I Am; to the Wonderful Counselor, Mighty God, Prince of Peace; to Emmanuel, which means "God with us." Jesus is always there to comfort, to heal, and to assure us that we are not alone.

Focus Verse: "Therefore, if anyone is in Christ, the new creation has come: The old has gone, the new is here!" ~ 2 Corinthians 5:17

Focus Prayer: Thank You, Lord, for changing us. We are sinners in need of a Savior, for all have sinned and fall short of the glory of God. Thank You for taking our old lives and making us new creations. May we walk in newness of life. In Jesus' Name, amen. (Romans 3:23, 2 Corinthians 5:17, Romans 6:4)

DAY 26

Remembering What He Has Promised:

His Promises Are True

Scripture tells us that all the promises of God are yes and amen. All the promises of God are mine through Christ. But I forget Him and His promises. And this tragic forgetfulness leaves me feeling powerless and poor.

I once heard a story about a homeless man who sat year after year on the streets of New York City, barely scraping by, living off the handouts of passersby. When he was found dead, obviously having perished due to the cold and exposure, the police were shocked to find about $30,000 in cash in his possession.

My husband's relative lived in fear of overdrawing his account each time he wrote a check. However, at his death, we discovered $75,000 in his checking account.

If I should receive a million dollars deposited into my checking account, what if I never wrote a check? What if I never took advantage of the gift? It would not change the fact that I was wealthy, but I certainly could still look and act like a pauper. And that is what Satan cunningly plans for us.

Our enemy does not want us to remember who we are and Whose we are. He does not want us to tap into the riches of God's promises. And he certainly does not want us to invest our riches in the lives of those around us, reaping a tremendous gain for the Kingdom of God. In fact, as long as he can keep us living with a slave mentality, we cannot reach our full royal status.

We need to sharpen our memories because we quickly forget God, His love, His power, His almighty dependability. We must remember that His promises are true.

Focus Verse: "For all the promises of God in Him are Yes, and in Him Amen, to the glory of God through us." 2 Corinthians 1:20 (NKJV)

Focus Prayer: Thank You, Lord, that though You were rich, You became poor so that through Your poverty on earth we may have the riches of heaven. Thank You that You are able to do immeasurably more than all we ask or imagine, according to Your power that is at work within us. In Jesus' Name, amen. (2 Corinthians 8:9, Ephesians 3:20)

DAY 27

Remember What He Has Instructed:

Praise

We adopted our daughter Sally from China in 2012. For having heard only Chinese for the first 22 months of her life, she did a remarkable job of learning English. When she had been with us for a year, I was convicted that it was time to teach her to pray. We had prayed over her daily for a year, but it was time for her to learn to say the words herself.

I was amazed with how she responded. We called her the "Prayer Police" because she directed us all in our dinnertime blessings. She made sure all heads were bowed, hands were folded, and eyes were closed. Of course, she had not clued in to the fact that the only reason she knew if someone was not complying was that she herself did not have her head bowed or her eyes closed.

At nighttime, we said our standard "God bless Mama, and Daddy, and Katie, and Ellie, and Joseph, and Troy, and Joshua. And God bless all my family and all my friends!"

She always had some particular person she wanted to add. "God bless Gran and D!" How did she know they were both sick? "God bless Uncle Martin!" How did she know he had a big presentation and needed extra prayer? "God bless Owen!" How did she know he needed extra encouragement? She just knew. She was not so busy with life to forget to listen, to forget to pray.

My favorite Sally-prayer began with her hands raised toward heaven with a heartfelt "I love you, Jesus!" Every night, that is the last thing she prayed. But then she began to add something precious to it: "I love you, Jesus! You're so cute!" Every night she said this to Jesus. It must have made Him smile.

She had learned the basics of praise—telling God who He is, not because *He* doesn't know who He is but as a way of telling Him that *we* know who He is. We taught our older kids to praise by filling in the following sentence: God, You are so _____ (holy, mighty, wonderful, faithful, great, powerful, kind, trustworthy, righteous, forgiving, merciful)!

Will you praise Him today? Will you tell Him who He is to you?

Focus Verse: "Praise the Lord, O my soul; all my inmost being, praise his holy name." ~ Psalm 103:1

Focus Prayer: We praise You, Lord, with everything in our inmost being. We praise You and do not forget all Your benefits. For you forgive our sins, heal us in every way, and redeem our lives from the pit of despair. Thank You, Lord, for satisfying our desires with good things so that our youth is renewed like the eagle's. May we glorify You with our lives. In Jesus' Name, amen. (Psalm 103:1–5)

DAY 28

Remember What He Has Instructed:

Serve Others

It was around 5 o'clock in the afternoon when my son Troy and I entered the library. Immediately, the wonderful smell of musty old books caused a wave of memories to pass over me. When I was a little girl, I used to walk to the library to check out books or attend the special programs offered there. When I was in high school, I went to the library for the resources needed for reports or research papers. When I was in college, I studied best in the stacks of the library. I have spent many hours in libraries over the years.

On this day, we were there for one purpose—to get a library card for Troy so that he could get five extra points in English class. As I looked around, I was surprised at the changes that had occurred since my library days. The center of the room held table after table of computers. Every one of them was occupied.

We chatted with the librarian as we waited for the card, and we were surprised to hear a loud scream break the quiet atmosphere. A four-year-old boy held tightly to a thin book as his mother pried it from his hands.

"But I want to take it!" he screamed.

"I will get it for you tomorrow, "she patiently said.

As they left, I thought what a good mom she was to bring him two days in a row to the library.

"Do they come here a lot?" I asked the librarian, who seemed to recognize the pair.

"Every day," she replied.

"Wow! Every day?"

"Every day, all day."

"All day?" I couldn't believe it.

"Yes, the Salvation Army makes them leave at 7:00 a.m., and they can return at 5:00 p.m."

"They're homeless?" I asked incredulously.

"Yes. Many of these people are homeless."

I shot a look around wondering which of the people surfing the internet didn't have a bed to sleep in at night. Homeless? In my perfect little town?

When we got in the car, I paused for a moment before I started the engine. I looked at Troy and said, "Honey, your mama is ridiculous." He gave me a look that said he didn't understand, so I continued. "I complain because I have to clean my house, but I have a house to clean. I complain because of the loads and loads of laundry I have to wash, but we have clothes to wash. I am ridiculous." He nodded like he understood and like he shared my sentiments for himself as well.

I pondered long and hard the following questions: What am I to do now? How will I let this tiny glimpse into the window of another's struggle change me? I am still trying to find practical ways to answer those questions. But I will continue to change. It would be ridiculous not to.

Focus Verse: "The King will reply, 'Truly I tell you, whatever you did for one of the least of these brothers and sisters of mine, you did for me.'" ~ Matthew 25:40

Focus Prayer: Lord, You tell us that we will always have opportunities to help others, for the poor will always be with us. We know that if we have the world's goods and see others in need, we must not close our hearts against them. As we help others, we show that the love of God abides in us. May we love one another, for love is from God, and everyone who loves is born of God and knows God. In Jesus' Name, amen. (Deuteronomy 15:11, 1 John 3:17, 1 John 4:7)

DAY 29

Remember What He Has Instructed:

Believe

We began this book with the story of Joshua gathering stones of remembrance from the Jordan River. At the Lord's command, Joshua said to the people, "In the future, when your children ask you, 'What do these stones mean?' tell them . . ." (Joshua 4:6–7). As a former teacher and a mother of seven, I know the children in our lives will ask about our faith, and we should prayerfully be prepared to tell them.

Years ago my niece Elizabeth went to see the Easter program at First Evangelical Church in Tupelo, Mississippi, where the church members put on an incredibly anointed drama of the story of Jesus. One climactic part was a scene in which Jesus, sitting on His throne of glory, is holding a large book. As He sees the joyful ones entering into the glorious heavenly realm, He marks off their names in the book.

That night, when my brother was putting Elizabeth to bed, she asked, "Daddy, what was that big book that Jesus was holding at the end of the play?"

"Why, Honey, that was the Book of Life. Jesus writes the names of all His followers—everyone who believes in Him and is going to heaven—in the Book of Life."

Elizabeth thought for a moment and then looked up at her dad and said, "I want my name in that book, Daddy." So they both knelt down beside her bed and took care of it then and there.

Do you remember when you first believed? Do you still believe?

According to the Merriam-Webster dictionary, to believe means "to consider to be true or honest; . . . to accept the word or evidence of."[5] Some of the synonyms of the word *believe* include *accept, trust, take,* and *swallow*.

Let me ask again. Do you believe? Do you accept the truth of the scriptures and trust that God is the Truth Teller and the Promise Keeper? Do you take His truth and swallow it? Psalm 34:8 says, "Taste and see that the LORD is good; blessed is the one who takes refuge in him."

I won't pretend that believing is always easy. Sometimes our believing is overshadowed by the circumstances in our lives, at which point we can pray like the man in the Bible who said, "I do believe; help me overcome my unbelief" (Mark 9:24).

Focus Verse: "For God so loved the world that he gave his one and only Son, that whoever believes in him shall not perish but have eternal life." ~ John 3:16

Focus Prayer: Thank You, Lord, that Your grace saves us. For it is by grace we have been saved through faith, and it is not from ourselves; it is a gift a God. We believe You, Lord. We believe Your Word. We believe You, but help us with our unbelief. In Jesus' Name, amen. (Ephesians 2:8, Mark 9:24)

DAY 30

Remember What He Has Instructed:

Be Still

Psalm 46:10 reminds us, "Be still, and know that I am God." As I recently dwelled on those words, I realized that this one verse embodies all three components of our life: the physical, the mental, and the spiritual.

It is in the physical realm that we can *be still*. We can all agree that it is hard to be still. I love my life! I would not choose to change a thing about it. But raising seven kids, trying to be a good wife, friend, and daughter, plus trying to run two companies, I am usually anything but still. It is hard for me to be still. I mean, don't other verses like 1 Corinthians 9:24 tell us to "run in such a way as to get the prize"? Yet we have been created to be still. We *need* to be still. Our society has lost the understanding of the importance of just being still.

I once read an article entitled "Where Have All the Front Porches Gone?" that described the shift in architectural design. Few houses these days include front porches. Why? Because no one has time to sit on one! No one has time to be still.

We must *learn* to be still. What does that look like practically? I really can't say what that looks like for you. Those are choices that you alone can make. But I do believe that it boils down to this: eliminate and concentrate. Eliminate those things that are unnecessary in your life. Concentrate on what matters—even if that means you have to go against the crowd. Give yourself wider margins in life. Don't fill up every second of every day. If you do, you will look back and realize that your days flew by in a blur and you will have missed the most valuable aspects of your life. And once missed, they can never be recouped.

Yes, we run the race to win the prize! Yes, we do our work heartily as Colossians 3:23 tells us. But just as importantly, we must carve out time to *be still*.

The Psalm tells us, "Be still and know that I am God." *Be still* is in the physical realm. *And know* is in the mental realm. What do you know? What is truth? So many lies bombard us all the time: "I am not good enough." "I am not efficient enough." "I am not gifted enough." What about this one? "I have messed up too badly to be redeemed." God's Word blows that lie out of the water and shouts the truth that no one and no situation is unredeemable.

We need to take our thoughts captive, as 2 Corinthians 10:5 says. We need to examine our thought processes. We need to quit believing lies about ourselves and instead commit to focusing only on things that are true and good and right. We need to know the truth, and we need to live like we know the truth.

What does the verse say? It says, "Be still, and know that I am God." *Be still* is in the physical realm. *And know* is in the mental realm. And *that I am God* is in the spiritual realm. We need to know that there is a powerful One who is on our side. God can bring the calm to our chaos. God can right our wrongs. God will never leave us nor forsake us.

Focus Verse: "Set your minds on things above, not on earthly things." ~ Colossians 3:2

Focus Prayer: May we be still and know that You, O Lord, are God. You will be exalted on the earth, in every nation. May we quiet our hearts, be still before You, and wait patiently for You to work. For we know that all things work for the good of those who love the Lord. And we love You, Lord. In Jesus' Name, amen. (Psalm 46:10, Psalm 37:7)

DAY 31

Remember What He Has Instructed:

Obey

It was bath time, a favorite time of day for Sally. At age three, she loved to splash and play in the warm water. She loved to "swim," play with foam letters, sing, and talk to herself. One particular day, she was having an especially fun time. She turned one of the foam letters into a doll, which she promptly put in time-out. I think it was the letter *H*. Poor guy. Unjustly accused.

I kept asking her if she was ready to get out, which was another way of saying, "It's time to wash your hair." She usually didn't mind this too much as she liked our little "Head Back, Eyes Closed" chant that we said over and over until all the soap was out.

But that day, she didn't want her hair washed. And she needed her hair washed. So she squirmed and wiggled and made it very difficult to lather up her beautiful black hair. Of course, "Head Back, Eyes Closed" doesn't help much when you are squirming. Soap will still get in your eyes. So I kept prompting her to be still so I could finish the task.

Just about the time I was ready to put her in time-out with letter *H*, she stopped squirming and put her head back with her eyes closed. I poured the water from a large cup and watched the soap run down her back far away from stingable eyes. And then she quietly said, "You're welcome, Mom."

At first, I thought it was cute. "Oh, what good manners," I almost let pass through my lips. Until I thought about it. "Wait a minute. She thinks she is doing me a favor?" What I was asking would only help her avoid a little pain.

And then it hit me. I do that to my Father. I wiggle and squirm when obedience to Him might not appeal to me at the time. And when I do obey, deep down do I think I am doing some great favor for Him? What He asks of me would only help me avoid a little (or a lot) of pain. Do I expect Him to thank me for obedience when instead I should thank Him for His gentle, consistent work in my life?

Sally and I finished with bath time and got to my favorite part. I wrapped her in a big, fluffy towel and held her tightly. And once again, I picked up another stone of remembrance offered to me by my sweet girl.

Focus Verse: "And this is love: that we walk in obedience to his commands." ~ 2 John 1:6

Focus Prayer: Lord, Your commands are sweet to our soul. May we be strong and very courageous, careful to obey all of Your laws. May we not turn from your commandments, so that we may be successful wherever we go. For we know that keeping your commandments shows our love for You. And we do love you, Lord. In Jesus' Name, amen. (Joshua 1:7, 1 John 5:3)

DAY 32

Remember What He Has Instructed:

Encourage One Another

"Mama! Mama!" Sally said over and over as I buckled her in her car seat. I admit I was distracted. But she was not deterred.

"Mama!" she yelled again.

"Yes, Sally?" I finally answered.

"I like your forehead, Mama. And your eyebrows!" she said in her sweetest voice.

"Well, thank you, Sally!" I said with a big smile. I was really trying hard not to laugh. I can't say I remember any-one ever complimenting my forehead or my eyebrows. Quite nice to hear, as I had embraced the middle-age rou-tine of creams and serums to try to fight off wrinkles.

I thought about her sweet words for weeks. In her funny, precious way, she encouraged me. She made my day, put a smile on my face, and gave me a fun memory to replay over and over, even when doubt and insecurity sometimes shout other things in my direction.

It made me think. How often could we make someone's day, put a smile on another's face, give someone encouragement to combat the doubt and insecurity shouting at them? A sincere, simple compliment has great power to build up another person in our daily path.

I then decided to listen to God more. Maybe He has a few things to say to others through me. I decided to see others as God sees them—a masterpiece that He took great pleasure in creating.

I decided to look people in the eye more often—not to pass by so quickly, eager to go on to the next thing on my list.

Soon after this, I found myself in the checkout line at Walmart. The *beep, beep, beep* sounded over and over again. A trip to Walmart for a family of twelve is quite an adventure. I watched the items go through one by one, and my thoughts wandered to the other errands left on my list. But then I remembered my new resolve. I looked up at the cashier and smiled. I asked her how her day was going. Though the lines on her face spoke of many years of hard work and maybe hard times, I saw the prettiest blue eyes.

"You have the prettiest eyes." The words spilled out before I could stop them. Before the question of "Will that sound weird?" affected my response. She smiled bigger and simply said, "Well, thank you." But I saw it. I saw that she was encouraged, that she felt a little bit happier. Once again, our little two-year-old taught me something God wanted me to remember.

Focus Verse: "Therefore encourage one another and build each other up." ~ 1Thessalonians 5:11

Focus Prayer: May we encourage one another and build each other up, not tear each other down. For by this everyone will know that we are Your disciples, if we love one another. Give us the fruit of the Spirit, which is love, joy, peace, patience, kindness, goodness, faithfulness, gentleness, and self-control. In Jesus' Name, amen. (1 Thessalonians 5:11, John 13:35, Galatians 5:22–23)

Remember What He Has Instructed:

Be Hospitable

After one of our Saturday Bible schools in Los Guidos, Costa Rica, my friend Kelli and I found ourselves in the home of a precious Costa Rican lady named Alicia. When she walked with her children to the huge tree in the center of sector 8, where we held our weekly program, she pulled me aside to invite us to come to her house after Bible school. We gladly accepted the invitation, although I must confess that I was a bit nervous. We did not know her very well, and at that point, we had never been invited to enter any of the dilapidated shacks that covered the mountainside.

As soon as all the other children had walked back to their own homes, we walked to Alicia's home with her three children. My eyes had to adjust a bit when we first entered. There was no electricity, so the only light was from the doorway and from a window that had been cut from the tin and wood-scrap walls. The home was just one room, which was partitioned by sheets hanging across rope attached to the ceiling.

Alicia excitedly welcomed us to her home. I noticed that the dirt floor had been neatly swept and all her meager belongings were in order. On the table were several broken glasses from several different patterns, a small plate full of saltine crackers, and a chipped pitcher of lemonade. There were no chairs for us to sit in, so we simply stood around the table and listened while she talked of her life and her love for the Lord. Such sweet fellowship of believers we experienced that day!

She offered us the crackers and lemonade, which we received with a gratitude that had nothing to do with the food and drink. I was overcome with her pure hospitality. Although we had been repeatedly warned against eating or drinking in that area because of unsanitary conditions, I took what was offered and silently prayed the prayer that my missionary friend Ben Pierce had once shared with me: "Lord, I'll get it down if You keep it down!"

When we were thanking her for her invitation and hospitality, she joyfully responded, "*Este es mi fiesta!*" (This is my party!) It was a party given in honor of us—a party given with grace and elegance despite the resources that she had to work with. Such pure hospitality and generosity I have rarely, if ever, seen since that day. And such conviction it brought to my soul. How many times do I resist reaching out to others because my house is not perfect or my dishes don't match or I don't have time to create an extravagant meal? And how many times do my guests leave my house feeling the joy of being honored, and the warmth of sweet fellowship?

After that day in Los Guidos, I am without excuses. I need to share my "party." The kingdom of God is a party to be shared with everyone we are privileged to come in contact with. And Scripture tells us that when we do it for "the least of these," we do it unto Him (Matthew 25:40). So whenever we reach out to anyone with a pure, loving heart, we are reaching up to Jesus. That shows extravagant love for Him.

Focus Verse: "Above all, love each other deeply, because love covers over a multitude of sins. Offer hospitality to one another without grumbling. Each of you should use whatever gift you have received to serve others, as faithful stewards of God's grace in its various forms." ~ 1 Peter 4:8–10

Focus Prayer: Lord, may we use our gifts and material goods to serve and bless others. May we love deeply, as we have been loved by You, O Lord. We know that You love a cheerful giver, so may we give generously and abundantly, for Your glory and not ours. In Jesus' Name, amen. (1 Peter 4:10, John 13:34, 2 Corinthians 9:7)

Remember What He Has Done:

He Said Yes

Driving down the road, I kept hearing the same muffled noise over and over. Sally had my cell phone and was replaying her favorite video of her and her brother Joshua. "Sally, what does Mama say?" Joshua asked over and over. Her response was always the same: "Honey, no!"

With each question her answer was more exaggerated. This little Asian girl has mastered the art of a Southern accent. "Hooonnneyyy, nooooo!" she said, with her eyes disappearing into tiny slits as her facial expressions supposedly mimicked mine.

I had to laugh. It was so funny to me that out of all the things I told her each day, that was what she remembered. Every day, countless times throughout the day, I told her

127

I loved her. I told her she was beautiful. I told her she was my angel and she was precious to me. I know she heard those things as well, but the first thing she remembered was "Hoooonnnneyyyy, noooooo!"

Many Christians view God the Father in the same way. We think of the all the nos He says. We focus on the don'ts instead of the dos. He often has to tell us, "Honey, no." But just as I say no to Sally because I love her and want her to be the best she can be, God the Father tells us no because He sees the end from the beginning. Father knows best.

But today I want to focus on all the many ways He says yes to us. In fact, I bet His yeses far outweigh His nos. He says yes to accepting us as we are, while gently leading us to higher ground. He says yes to forgiving our sins over and over and over again. He says yes to countless blessings, though He knows we may not even notice them. He says yes to redeeming our worst to make it our best.

He says yes to making us, the bound slaves of sin, into His treasured sons and daughters. He says yes to all the promises in His Word offered to an undeserving people. He said yes to sacrificing His one and only Son. He said yes to watching Him suffer and die in agony. He said yes to His Sacrificial Lamb being the payment for our sins.

He said yes, so doesn't it make sense for us to say yes to Him? Will you say yes today?

Focus Verse: "My son, do not make light of the Lord's discipline, and do not lose heart when he rebukes you, because the Lord disciplines the one he loves, and he chastens everyone he accepts as his son." ~ Hebrews 12:5–6

Focus Prayer: Lord, may we accept Your discipline when we need it. May we not run from it but embrace it. For we know that You correct the ones You love, as a father who corrects a son he loves. Teach us to number our days so that we can gain a heart of wisdom. In Jesus' Name, amen. (Hebrews 12:6, Proverbs 3:12, Psalm 90:12)

Remember What He Has Done:

He Calls Us by Name

When we first adopted Sally, we discovered that she loved names. It's so ironic because for the first 22 months of her life, she didn't really have a name. She was more of a number in the vast orphanage system. She was assigned a "name" in the orphanage, but part of that name was simply an abbreviated part of the name of the city where the orphanage was located. Her last name was "Yang" because her orphanage was in Yangchun City. For the first 22 months of her life she was identified by where she was, not who she was. And where she was was a sad place. I hate that she was identified by that sad place instead of by the joyful girl she truly is.

On March 9, 2012, she officially became our daughter and a U.S. citizen, and she was officially given a new, real name—Sara Ruth Berry.

My daughter loved names. As a two-year-old, in most every sentence she said, she included the name of the person she was addressing. "I'm hungry, Mama." "I go play, Mama?" "Mama, mook at me!" "Who's dat, Mama?" "What's dat, Mama?" She wanted to know the name of everyone and everything. And once she was told the name of anyone or anything, she usually remembered it.

My daughter loves names. So does her Heavenly Father. She is now old enough to understand that He calls her by name. God says, "Do not fear, for I have redeemed you; I have summoned you by name; you are mine" (Isaiah 43:1).

I can't wait for her—and all of us—to experience God's delightful surprise He has for us when we get to heaven. Revelation 2:17 tells us that He will give us a special gift—a beautiful white stone. And with that gift, He will give us a holy nickname, known just between the two of us.

Sally will love that! She loves names.

Focus Verse: "Whoever has ears, let them hear what the Spirit says to the churches. To the one who is victorious, I will give some of the hidden manna. I will also give that person a white stone with a new name

written on it, known only to the one who receives it."
~ Revelation 2:17

Focus Prayer: Thank You, Lord, that You have created and formed us. We are fearfully and wonderfully made. We have nothing to fear because You, Lord, have redeemed us and called us by name. We are Yours, Lord, forever. We praise You for this great truth. In Jesus' Name, amen. (Psalm 139:14, Isaiah 43:1)

DAY 36

Remember What He Has Done:

He Has Accomplished Everything

I have had the privilege of witnessing the beauty of the unity of the Body of Christ. When I was living in Costa Rica, we went for a weekend to a Young Life Camp called "La Vida." *La Vida* means "The Life," and what an accurate description that was! Beautiful life was everywhere: in the indescribable beach setting, in the countenance of the people, and in the message they proclaimed.

The director of La Vida, Marv Asphalt, led us in a beautiful Sabbath service right on the beach. I found myself surrounded by all different kinds of people from all different walks of life. There was a youth group from the United States who had an incredible heart for worship. There were the Asphalts, who had committed their lives to missions and to leading young people to Christ. There were Costa Rican La Vida staff members who had also devoted their lives to spreading the gospel. There was a Costa Rican Catholic priest who ran the orphanage next to La Vida. And there were lots and lots of beautiful Costa Rican children, bound to each other because of the common lot of being orphans.

We all came together with all of our differences and worshiped in unity. We were allowed the gift of witnessing a historic event. It was the first time that Marv, who was a Methodist minister, and the Catholic priest had come together to share the Sabbath. They stood side by side and broke the communion bread together, reminding us of the broken body of our Lord. Marv spoke of the body of Christ—of the unity of the body, and of breaking down the divisions in the body. Together, they served the group. Each person received a special blessing as they were served. It was if the focus were totally on that person. It brought to mind the reality that the cross was a personal gift to each one of us. If I were the only one who needed saving, Christ still would have died for me. Incredible yet true!

Marv knelt before each of the orphaned children and looked each one in the eye, explaining that the broken body of the King of kings was a gift for each of them and that we are all orphans until we are adopted into the family of God, whereby we cry, Abba! Father! Daddy!

When all had been served, Marv lifted the remaining bread toward heaven. With tears streaming down his face, he said in a loud voice, "It is finished!"

"It is finished" (John 19:30). Our Savior spoke those words from the cross, just before He died for us. "It is finished." Nothing more needs to be done. He did it all for us. We don't deserve it. We can't earn it. Jesus bought it for us. And it is free—the completed work of Christ offered as a gift to our weary, lost, and orphaned souls. The body was broken once and for all. Communion is a reminder of that. We do not need to break the body again, as we often do through our divisions and pettiness and self-righteousness. In the high priestly prayer, the last before His betrayal, our Lord included a call to unity:

> My prayer is not for them alone. I pray also for those who will believe in me through their message, that all of them may be one, Father, just as you are in me and I am in you. May they also be in us so that the world may believe that you have sent me. . . . so that they may be brought to complete unity. Then the world will know that you sent me and have loved them even as you have loved me. (John 17:20–21, 23)

Focus Verse: "His divine power has given us everything we need for a godly life through our knowledge of him who called us by his own glory and goodness." ~ 2 Peter 1:3

Focus Prayer: Lord, thank You for finishing the great work of the cross. Thank You that because it is finished, we can live eternally and abundantly. Thank You for the free gift of Your grace, by which we are saved. We love You and praise You for You are the King of ages, immortal, invisible, the only true God. To You be honor and glory forever. In Jesus' Name, amen. (John 19:30, Ephesians 2:8, John 17:3, 1 Timothy 1:17)

DAY 37

Remember What He Has Done:

He Forgave

On the day of the Resurrection of our Lord and Savior, three women rose early. They had a mission. The law would not let them fulfill their mission until dawn, so they set out just as the sun began to rise. They took spices to anoint the bruised body of the One they adored.

What did they see? They saw an angel in a white robe. The angel said what angels always say: "Don't be afraid." And then, as usual, the angel issued a call to respond, a command. Go. Go and tell. And so it is with us. We must overcome fear. We must go. We must tell. Who we tell depends on what He tells us to do. But we all must go. We all must tell.

Who were these particular women supposed to tell? The disciples . . . and Peter. Poor, poor Peter. He was still deeply wounded from the greatest failure of his life. I'm sure the memory of the sound of the cock's crow haunted him over and over in the waking hours and filled his mind with troubled dreams at night. And yet the angel said, "But go, tell his disciples and Peter" (Mark 16:7).

I envision the scene like this: The women, amazed and overwhelmed, rush into the room where the disciples are hiding and grieving together. They are talking all at once, laughing and crying, creating such a commotion that the disciples are confused. Peter, still filled with grief and shame, stands detached in the corner. When he hears "He's not there! He has risen!" he rushes forward to hear more clearly. But then he hears something else—that same cock's crow haunting his mind and spirit once again. He turns back to the corner, head down, thinking, "Even if it is true, He wouldn't want to see me." Shame, guilt, and regret threaten to break his heart once again.

One of the other disciples finally halts the commotion of women laughing and crying, and men begin shouting all their questions at once. When at last there is a pause, he says, "Slow down. Tell us slowly. Tell us exactly what he said."

One of the women rises to the position of spokesperson and says, "There was a man in a white robe. He said, 'Tell his disciples and Peter. . . .'"

At the sound of his name, the cock's crow becomes silent. "He called me by name! He wants me to know that

He has risen. Then he must forgive me. He is alive!" And with that we see the first recorded occurrence of the power of the resurrection. He lives. And He forgives.

And what was Peter's reaction? He took off running toward the Savior. He searched for Him with all his heart. And it was upon this forgiven rock that Jesus built His church. The revival in Peter's heart had begun. And it would ignite revival throughout the world.

We need another revival, don't we? Do you hear him call your name? Listen carefully. He is calling you. And your name, whispered through His holy lips, will silence those horrible thoughts of sin, shame, and insecurity. Let this truth bring revival to your own heart. Then go and tell.

Focus Verse: "Do not fear, for I have redeemed you; I have summoned you by name; you are mine." ~ Isaiah 43:1

Focus Prayer: Oh, what manner of love You, the Father, have lavished on us! That we are called the children of God is more than we could have ever hoped for, given our lowly, sinful state. We know that when Christ appears, we will be like Him, for we shall see Him as He is. Having this great hope, help us to purify ourselves, just as Christ is pure. In Jesus' Name, amen. (1 John 3:1–3)

DAY 38

Remember What He Has Done:

He Crushed the Enemy's Head

I once heard a sermon that mapped out the last journeys of Jesus. Do you know where his last stop was before he entered Jerusalem, which He knew would lead to agony and death? He went to see His dear friends Mary, Martha, and Lazarus.

Why did He want to spend his last days with these three? While I can't pretend to know the motivations of Jesus, I can imagine what He may have felt. Think about where you would want to go if you knew you were about to die. You would go where you knew you were loved. Jesus went where He would be loved extravagantly. And that extravagant love would usher in the resurrection power of the risen Christ. We find the story in John 12:1–8.

Six days before the Passover, Jesus came to Bethany, where Lazarus lived, whom Jesus had raised from the dead. Here a dinner was given in Jesus' honor. Martha served, while Lazarus was among those reclining at the table with him. Then Mary took about a pint of pure nard, an expensive perfume; she poured it on Jesus' feet and wiped his feet with her hair. And the house was filled with the fragrance of the perfume. But one of his disciples, Judas Iscariot, who was later to betray him, objected, "Why wasn't this perfume sold and the money given to the poor? It was worth a year's wages." He did not say this because he cared about the poor but because he was a thief; as keeper of the money-bag, he used to help himself to what was put into it. "Leave her alone," Jesus replied. "It was intended that she should save this perfume for the day of my burial. You will always have the poor among you, but you will not always have me."

Looking at the passage, we must ask ourselves what extravagant love looks like. They showed their love for Jesus by welcoming and honoring Him. They showed their love for Jesus in the way they spent their money. They showed their love for Jesus by their willingness to be misunderstood and ridiculed because of Him. They showed their love for Jesus by being willing to serve Him in humility.

Mary fell at Jesus' feet—a sign of respect and awe. And she ceremonially washed His feet, which was the job of a servant or slave. Mary wiped His feet with her hair. In those days a women's hair was her personal glory. When Mary let her hair down to wipe His feet, she was communicating two things. She was saying, "Lord, I give all my glory to You, for You alone are worthy." And she was saying, "I don't care what others think. I am willing to appear foolish in expressing my love to my Lord." That is extravagant love.

Others also enjoyed the fruit of Mary's extravagant love. Note that "the house was filled with the fragrance of the perfume" (John 12:3). When we love Jesus in an extravagant way, the overflow of that love spreads to others.

Most significantly, we see that Mary showed her love for Jesus by anointing His feet. It was more customary to anoint the head. In many passages of the Bible, we find that the head was anointed to signify a prophet, like Elijah or Elisha. And anointing of the head was especially important in anointing a king, like David or Solomon. But nothing could make Jesus more of a king. He was already King of kings when He was lying in a manger. The shepherds worshipped Him as king, and the wise men brought him king-worthy gifts. What needed anointing were His feet, for He had a long, painful journey ahead of Him.

He had to walk the hill of Calvary. He had to have those anointed feet nailed to a cross. But most importantly, His feet were anointed for burial, because through death, His anointed feet would fulfill the very first prophecy of the coming Messiah.

> So the LORD God said to the serpent [Satan, who had tricked Eve], "Because you have done this, 'Cursed are you above all the livestock and all the wild animals! You will crawl on your belly and you will eat dust all the days of your life. [Here comes the first prophecy!] And I will put enmity between you and the woman, and between your offspring and hers; he [Eve's future offspring, Jesus!] will crush your head, and you will strike his heel.'" (Genesis 3:14–15. Commentary in brackets is mine.)

You see, Jesus would use those anointed feet to spiritually stomp Satan's head, forever giving victory to all who believe!

We will spend a lot of our time in eternity at those anointed feet, falling down at His feet, casting our crowns at His feet. Why don't we just go ahead and start loving Him extravagantly like that now, worshipping Him with all our hearts and souls and minds and time and resources and homes?

After I thought about what it looked like to love Jesus extravagantly, I had to ask myself: Would Jesus have come to my house? Do I show extravagant love for Him? Would He have come to your house?

It is significant that Jesus stayed in Bethany for six days. On the seventh day, He entered Jerusalem. Remember that seven is the biblical number for completion and perfection. Everything was fulfilled that needed to take place before the ultimate sacrifice began. And the last thing needed was the anointing for burial, which Mary fulfilled through her extravagant display of love. Once we come to the place of surrender and extravagant love, then we are prepared to see an extraordinary God work mightily in our ordinary lives.

Focus Verse: "Therefore, I urge you, brothers and sisters, in view of God's mercy, to offer your bodies as a living sacrifice, holy and pleasing to God—this is your true and proper worship. Do not conform to the pattern of this world, but be transformed by the renewing of your mind. Then you will be able to test and approve what God's will is—his good, pleasing and perfect will." ~ Romans 12:1-2

Focus Prayer: Because of Your great mercy toward us, Lord, we offer ourselves as a living sacrifice. May we be holy and acceptable to you. Help us not to be conformed to the standards of this world, but help us to instead be transformed by the renewing of our minds. In Jesus' Name, amen. (Romans 12:1-2)

Remember What He Has Done:

He Wore the Thorns

My grandmother was a precious and godly woman. One of her greatest pleasures was growing a yard full of beautiful roses, the majority of which she gave away to others. I remember seeing buckets and buckets of roses in her kitchen as she prepared to share them. Only recently I learned that she went a step further than just being generous; she spent hours removing the thorns of every rose she gave away. She wanted her friends and family to enjoy the beauty of the roses without the pain of the thorns. She endured all the pricks for them.

As we celebrate—and grieve—the great sacrifice of Jesus, we should remember that He took the curse of thorns on His holy head so we wouldn't have to. We find from Genesis 3:18 and Numbers 33:55 that in the Holy Land, the ground was cursed with prickly thorns.

Often we become aware of thorns in our lives. These may be "thorns of the flesh" like Paul had:

> Therefore, in order to keep me from becoming conceited, I was given a thorn in my flesh, a messenger of Satan, to torment me. Three times I pleaded with the Lord to take it away from me. But he said to me, "My grace is sufficient for you, for my power is made perfect in weakness." Therefore I will boast all the more gladly about my weaknesses, so that Christ's power may rest on me. (2 Corinthians 12:7–9)

Do you have thorns to deal with right now? We all will at one point or another in our spiritual journeys. These can be a constant source of irritation, temptation, or pain. As Paul discovered when he asked for his thorn to be removed, God is enough. God's power is made perfect in our weak, thorn-filled situations. We must realize that every thorn allowed in our life is filtered through His great love. Every thorn has already pierced Him before it ever reaches us.

What are we supposed to do with these thorns? Turn to Jesus. He took the curse of thorns on Himself when He allowed the crown of thorns on His holy head. And when the curse is gone, the healing can begin.

Consider the beautiful truth laid out in the following poem by Martha Snell Nicholson.

The Thorn

I stood a mendicant of God before His royal throne.

And begged him for one priceless gift, which I could call my own.

I took the gift from out His hand, but as I would depart.

I cried, "But Lord this is a thorn and it has pierced my heart.

This is a strange, a hurtful gift, which Thou hast given me."

He said, "My child, I give good gifts and gave My best to thee."

I took it home and though at first the cruel thorn hurt sore,

As long years passed I learned at last to love it more and more.

I learned He never gives a thorn without this added grace,

He takes the thorn to pin aside the veil which hides His face.[6]

Through every difficulty, every thorn of our flesh and soul, God is our ever-present help. He will never leave us or forsake us. In these truths we can rest.

Focus Verse: "Now we see things imperfectly, like puzzling reflections in a mirror, but then we will see everything with perfect clarity. All that I know now is partial and incomplete, but then I will know everything completely, just as God now knows me completely." ~ 1 Corinthians 13:12 (NLT)

Focus Prayer: Thank You, Lord, that You rescue us from every miry pit and give us a firm place to stand. Thank You that Your grace is sufficient for us and even in our weakness we can experience Your power. Thank you for Your love and mercy toward us, which are never-ending. Because of Your great love for us we are not consumed by our problems, for Your compassions never fail. They are new every morning; great is Your faithfulness. In Jesus' Name, amen. (Psalm 40:2, 2 Corinthians 12:9, Lamentations 3:22–23)

DAY 40

Remember What He Has Done:

He Said Yes

One beautiful example of revival took place twenty years ago, and its story began with one ill-equipped couple, Mark and Gloria Zook. Ironically, their story began with a call heard only by them. No one else seemed to hear it or even to believe that they had heard it. Mission board after mission board refused to accept their applications, saying they were too old and not healthy enough to be missionaries. Finally, their home church responded to their call and sent them under their leadership.

Once they began living with the New Guinea tribe, the Zooks spent months chronologically telling the stories of the Old Testament, pointing out all the moments that foreshadowed Christ. When they got to the part about

Abraham sacrificing Isaac, they ended the day's storytelling with Isaac on the altar. They waited till the next day to tell the ending.

The people pondered and discussed what they thought would happen. Four different men came to Mr. Zook and said, "Abraham was a godly man, so he must obey God. God promised a savior through Isaac, so Isaac must be spared. God will send a substitute lamb." It was this story that made the connection when the Zooks taught the New Guinea tribe about the crucifixion and resurrection. They understood that Jesus was the substitute Lamb.

When this truth sank in, something truly amazing happened. Many began to shout "EE-Taow," which means, "It is true! It is very true and good!" Though these people were normally reserved, spontaneous celebration broke out and lasted for two and a half hours. They laughed and shouted "EE-Taow" over and over. They picked up Mr. Zook, the one rejected by mission boards as too old and too sick for ministry, and carried him on their shoulders in celebration.

EE-Taow! It is true! The story of Jesus and His love is true! We may not react in the same way, but we, too, can experience revival. We may be too reserved to jump up and down, but I at least want you to feel that on the inside. EE-Taow! It is true!

And what are we going to do about it? We can be used to ignite the fires of revival in our country. As my friend the Reverend Maxie Dunnam says, "It is not great men who change the world, but weak men in the hands of a great God." Are you willing to bring your weakness to our great God? Are you willing to be revived?

I once shared this at a women's retreat, and as I spoke, I pictured the scene in New Guinea. I felt myself getting emotional, so I thought I had better end it quickly. I closed by saying, "EE-Taow! It's true! And what are we going to do about it?" Then I invited anyone who wanted to pray to come to the hallway to pray with one of the prayer team members. I watched an eighty-year-old woman hobble over to one of the prayer team members and fall into her arms. She was crying and saying over and over, "What are we going to do about it? What are we going to do about it?" Eighty years old and still pressing on, wanting to be used, wanting to be revived.

We need to know: It's not over till it's over. And it's not over until God says it's over. And until that day comes when He calls us home, we should spend all of our best energy doing whatever He calls us to do in reaction to the truth that He lives and He forgives.

Just as Paul prayed for his beloved Ephesian brothers and sisters, so I pray for you, my dear friends, this verse: "I keep asking that the God of our Lord Jesus Christ, the glorious Father, may give you the Spirit of wisdom and revelation, so that you may know him better" (Ephesians 1:17).

Focus Verse: "Therefore God exalted him to the highest place and gave him the name that is above every name, that at the name of Jesus every knee should bow, in heaven and on earth and under the earth, and every tongue acknowledge that Jesus Christ is Lord, to the glory of God the Father." ~ Philippians 2:9–11

Focus Prayer: Jesus, you are everything to us. In You we live and move and exist. Apart from You we can do nothing. We bow our knee to You alone, Jesus, and our tongues acknowledge that You, Jesus, are Lord of Lords and King of kings. We love You. In Jesus' Name, amen. (Acts 17:28, Philippians 2:9–11, Revelation 17:14)

CONCLUSION

When we began this book, we found Joshua gathering stones of remembrance. The Lord wanted the Israelites to take stones from the River Jordan because He knew so well that they were a forgetful people. They were forgetful about who He is, what He can do, and what He requires. And for the rest of Joshua's life, he was called to remember. Joshua's gathering of the stones from Jordan was just the beginning.

Throughout his time of leadership, Joshua was called to gather stones of remembrance seven different times. The seventh time was just before his death. This is found in Joshua 23 and 24.

> After a long time had passed and the Lord had given Israel rest from all their enemies around them, Joshua, by then a very old man, summoned all Israel—their elders, leaders, judges and officials—and said to them: "I am very old. You yourselves have seen everything the Lord your God has done to all

these nations for your sake; it was the Lᴏʀᴅ your God who fought for you. Remember. . . ." (Joshua 23:1–4)

And then Joshua began to instruct the people for the last time. This is what he told them:

Be very strong: be careful to obey all that is written in the Book of the Law of Moses, without turning aside to the right or to the left. (Joshua 23:6)

Compare that to what Joshua heard over and over from the Lord himself, when he first became leader:

Be strong and very courageous. Be careful to obey all the law my servant Moses gave you; do not turn from it to the right or to the left, that you may be successful wherever you go. . . . Have I not commanded you? Be strong and courageous. Do not be afraid; do not be discouraged, for the Lᴏʀᴅ your God will be with you wherever you go. (Joshua 1:7, 9)

Joshua passed the wisdom, which had now been tested and proved, on to the others. He then gave more instruction:

But you are to hold fast to the Lᴏʀᴅ your God, as you have until now. The Lᴏʀᴅ has driven out before you great and powerful nations; to this day no one has been able to withstand you. One of you routs a thousand, because the LORD your God fights for you, just as he promised. So be very careful to love the LORD your God. . . . You know with all your heart and soul that not one of all the good promises the LORD your God gave you has failed. Every promise has been fulfilled; not one has failed. (Joshua 23:8–11, 14)

He then gathered all the people together and called them to remember the great journey on which God had led them. He challenged them, through remembering, to renew their covenant. He said:

Choose for yourselves this day whom you will serve. . . . But as for me and my household, we will serve the LORD. (Joshua 24:15)

The people renewed their covenant to their faithful God, and then Joshua called them to action. They were to do two things:

1. They were to rid themselves of all false gods.
2. They were to yield their hearts to the Lord.

And the people enthusiastically agreed. Joshua drew up a plan of obedience and then took a large stone and set it up under an oak tree as a stone of remembrance of their renewed covenant.

This proved to be Joshua's last assignment from God. He died just after setting up this final stone of remembrance. With this seventh stone, Joshua could rest. Seven being the number of completeness and perfection signified that with this last stone, Joshua had completed his ministry. This sounds much like what Paul wrote in 2 Timothy 4:7: "I have fought the good fight, I have finished the race, I have kept the faith."

With these seven different piles of stones of remembrance scattered throughout the land, the land itself shouted the story of God's faithful promises: the wonderful Promised Land. This helps us understand with greater clarity the encounter with Jesus found in Luke 19:37–40:

> When he came near the place where the road goes down the Mount of Olives, the whole crowd of disciples began joyfully to praise God in loud voices for all the miracles they had seen: "Blessed is the king who comes in the name of the Lord!" "Peace in heaven and glory in the highest!" Some of the Pharisees in the crowd said to Jesus, "Teacher, rebuke your disciples!" "I tell you," he replied, "if they keep quiet, the stones will cry out."

Throughout his years of stone gathering, Joshua learned above all to remember who God is, what He has done, and what He can do—to remember that He is an extraordinary God who loves to work in the lives of ordinary people.

It is the stones of remembrance—the remembering—that will especially give us strength through every season of our faith walk. And that is what life is all about—remembering that in our ordinary lives, there is a living, active, and extraordinary God!

ABOUT THE AUTHOR

Sara W. Berry has been teaching in classrooms and churches for over thirty-five years. Her experience began at Millsaps College in Jackson, Mississippi, where she received a Bachelor of Science Degree in Education, as well as numerous education and leadership awards.

Sara taught elementary students in Memphis, TN; Nashville, TN; Jackson, MS; Costa Rica; and Ecuador. She was director of a tutorial program for inner-city children in Jackson, MS, as well as program director for an inner-city humanitarian service in Memphis, TN. She also served as children's director for her church in Tupelo, MS.

Sara has an intense love for discipleship. She desires to teach, through her books and curriculum, the truth of God's Word, knowing that the Word does not return void. Sara has an equal passion for missions. She has taken seriously the mandate of the Great Commission, having ministered in Costa Rica, Ecuador, Peru, Nicaragua, and China.

With the gift of teaching and a passion for discipleship, Sara finds great joy in sharing the truth of the Scriptures with others. She has spoken to thousands of women from the United States, South America, and China.

Sara has written numerous books and curricula for children and adults, including the award-winning character-building series Integrity Time, award-winning children's book *Summer of 1969*, and best-selling book *Tap Code*, cowritten with Colonel Smitty Harris.

She is married to Dr. Mont Berry. They have seven children and three children-in-law: Katie and Owen, Ellie and Drew, Joseph, Troy and Rorie, Joshua, Sally, and Charlie.

Please visit her website, www.sarawberry.com.

NOTES

1. Lyrics.com, STANDS4 LLC, 2021. "Come, Thou Fount of Every Blessing Lyrics." Accessed January 18, 2021. https://www.lyrics.com/lyric/5103403

2. Kay Arthur, *Our Covenant God* (Colorado Springs: WaterBrook Multnomah, 1999), 3, Kindle.

3. Dr. and Mrs. Howard Taylor, *Hudson Taylor's Spiritual Secret*, 108, Kindle.

4. Lexico.com, s.v. "dwell," accessed January 16, 2021, https://www.lexico.com/en/definition/dwell

5. *Merriam-Webster Online*, s.v. "believe," accessed January 2, 2021, https://www.merriam-webster.com/dictionary/believe

6. Martha Snell Nicholson, "The Thorn," accessed January 16, 2021, https://www.thegospelcoalition.org/blogs/justin-taylor/the-thorn/

A free ebook edition
is available with the
purchase of this book.

To claim your free ebook edition:

1. Visit MorganJamesBOGO.com
2. Sign your name CLEARLY in the space
3. Complete the form and submit a photo of
   the entire copyright page
4. You or your friend can download the ebook
   to your preferred device

Print & Digital Together Forever.

Snap a photo

Free ebook

Read anywhere